HEALTHY
Instant Pot®
COOKBOOK

Use of the trademarks is authorized by DOUBLE INSIGHT Inc., owner of Instant Pot®

HEALTHY
Instant Pot®
COOKBOOK

Dana Angelo White, MS, RD, ATC

ALPHA

Table of Contents

Introduction

I've been using a pressure cooker since I was a little girl, only back then it was a stovetop model that could explode all over the kitchen at any minute. In recent years, pressure cookers have gotten a reboot, and not only are electric pressure cookers easier and safer to use, they come equipped with added features to allow for all kinds of healthy cooking. From yogurt to soups, to rice to pasta, to ribs and chicken, I use the Instant Pot multiple times a week for make-ahead meal prep and effortless weeknight dinners. I designed *Healthy Instant Pot Cookbook* for people like me—busy folks who want to make healthy, homemade meals, despite being pressed for time. No matter where you are on your pressure cooker journey—whether you're using your Instant Pot daily, or you're still building up the courage to take it out of the box—this book is for you. In these pages you'll find step-by-step recipes, full nutrition information, and tips and tricks to help you transform whole, seasonal ingredients into healthy meals in your Instant Pot that will wow your family and guests.

Dana White

Dana Angelo White, MS, RD, ATC

Author Acknowledgments

The inspiration for my recipes comes from numerous places, but particularly from my family. I grew up in a house where some of the happiest moments were centered around cooking and eating together. Today, family recipes and nostalgic flavors from both the Angelo and White sides of the family are often the foundation for new recipes. These traditions are shaping the food landscape for my three daughters, and I wouldn't want it any other way. I am also lucky to have a strong support system outside of my home kitchen—my colleagues at Quinnipiac University, many of whom I've convinced to buy Instant Pots while working on this book, and my tight knit "framily" of friends in the community of Fairfield where I live. Thank you all for encouraging me to play with food and share it with you. Finally, *Healthy Instant Pot Cookbook* would not exist without the team at DK Books lead by Brook Farling. I so appreciate your expertise and ability to turn my delicious (and sometimes scattered) ideas into properly organized realities.

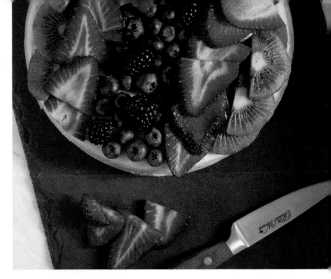

About the Author

Dana Angelo White, MS, RD, ATC is a registered dietitian, certified athletic trainer, author, journalist, and nutrition and fitness consultant. She specializes in culinary nutrition, recipe development, and sports nutrition. She is the nutrition expert for FoodNetwork.com, and is a founding contributor to the Food Network's *Healthy Eats* blog. Dana is the sports dietitian for the D-1 athletic program and assistant clinical faculty in the Department of Athletic Training and Sports Medicine at Quinnipiac University in Hamden, Connecticut. Her work has been featured on FoodNetwork.com, Verywell.com, CookingLight.com, and in Today's Dietitian, SHAPE, SEVENTEEN, Prevention, Muscle & Fitness, Men's Fitness, and Maxim. Dana is the author of *Healthy Air Fryer Cookbook* (Alpha, 2017), *First Bites: Superfoods for Babies and Toddlers* (TarcherPerigee, 2015), and *Healthy Quick & Easy Smoothies* (Alpha, 2018).

Instant Pot® Basics

Introducing the Instant Pot®

Before the Instant Pot you needed separate appliances to pressure cook, slow cook, steam, sauté, and bake, but now it can all be done with this unique, all-in-one multicooker appliance. The Instant Pot will change how you cook.

What's all the Fuss?

A traditional pressure cooker is a wonderful kitchen tool to own. It can render tough cuts of meat tender and cook vegetables perfectly—all in a fraction of the time it takes with other methods and appliances. But if you've ever been around a traditional pressure cooker, a few things quickly become apparent: there's a whole lot of noise, and there's also a lingering feeling that the top could blow at any moment.

Well, the Instant Pot isn't your grandmother's pressure cooker—it's different, and it's more. It's a multi-purpose appliance that, in addition to pressure cooking, can bake, sauté, steam, slow cook, and even function as a rice cooker and yogurt maker. There's no rattling pressure regulator on top of the cooker—it's quiet, and it includes a number of pre-set cooking programs that are each designed and precision-tuned to cook specific types of foods to exact times and temperatures. Remember when you had to sauté food prior to placing it in a slow cooker? You can sauté food right in the Instant Pot. And that slow cooker? You'll no longer need it, because the Instant Pot is also a fully functional slow cooker. The Instant Pot serves as an excellent rice cooker, as well, and it's the perfect yogurt maker. The pre-set programs enable you to cook nearly any type of food. (You can even bake a cake!) And if you're a home canner, the Instant Pot is the perfect home-canning appliance for sterilizing and pressurizing. You can even use it as a food warmer.

There is a bit of a learning curve to mastering the Instant Pot, but after a quick orientation and a few recipes, you'll be thrilled with how this unique appliance transforms your cooking, and you'll find that you no longer need so many other appliances in your kitchen.

How is it better?

Why else does the Instant Pot belong in your kitchen? Here are a few more good reasons.

It cooks fast

The Instant Pot cooks faster than other forms of cooking, and it does it better. Pressure cooking creates an environment that cooks food quickly and evenly. Cooking this way is faster than conventional methods, and in many instances the cooking times in the Instant Pot are half of those of other methods.

It cooks healthier

The longer food is cooked, the more nutrients can be lost in the cooking process. The high heat, rapid cooking times, and pressurization of pressure cooking help retain more nutrients in the foods you cook.

It's energy efficient

Because you're using fewer burners on a stove, and taking less time to prepare your food, you're also using less energy. As a general rule, the Instant Pot uses significantly less energy than many common appliances.

A variety of models

The Instant Pot comes in a variety of models including the Duo, Duo Plus, Lux, Ultra, Smart, and Max, and they come in a variety of sizes, with the most popular sizes being the 6- and 8-quart models, as well as a smaller 3-quart model. (The recipes in this book were made using the 6-quart Instant Pot Duo 60.)

Note that depending on which model you own, you may notice some subtle differences in the organization of the controls, as well as the names of some of the programs. Some older models may have a **Manual** program button, which is the equivalent of the **Pressure Cook** button on most newer models. Some older models may also have a **Start** button, while the programs on newer models may start automatically, with programs beginning 10 seconds after the program has been selected.

Instant Pot® Programs and Controls

The Instant Pot features an incredible range of cooking programs and controls, many of which can be adjusted for whatever the desired cooking result may be.

The Control Panel

The control panel is the nerve center of the Instant Pot and contains the LCD screen, as well as all of the controls, indicators, and program keys you'll use to control the pot.

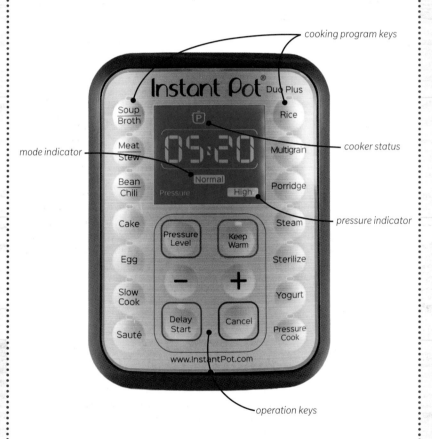

cooking program keys

mode indicator

cooker status

pressure indicator

operation keys

Mode Indicators

The mode indicators enable you to control the results by adjusting the total cooking time for the selected cooking program. The mode can be adjusted by pressing a program button repeatedly until the desired mode is selected.

LESS: Reduces the overall cooking time for any preset cooking program.

NORMAL: The factory default cooking time for all preset cooking programs.

MORE: Increases the overall cooking time for any preset cooking program.

Pressure Indicators

The pressure indicators signal that a pressure program has been selected, and also show the amount of pressure being used in the program.

PRESSURE: Indicates that the Instant Pot is powered on, and a pressure cooking program has been selected.

LOW: Indicates that a pressure mode has been selected, and the pressure level has been adjusted to low.

HIGH: Indicates that a pressure mode has been selected, and the pressure level has been adjusted to high.

Cooker Status Icons

The cooker status icons are simply visual indicators that show the cooking status of the Instant Pot. Which icons are illuminated during a cooking program will depend on which program has been selected.

COOKING: The cooking icon indicates that the pot is on, a cooking program has been selected, and the pot is heating up, or is at full temperature.

 PRESSURE COOK: The pressure cook icon indicates that a pressure cooking program has been selected, and pressure is building in the pot.

 WARM: The warm icon indicates that a cooking program has been completed, and the Keep Warm function has been activated.

SOUND OFF: The sound off icon indicates that the sounds have been turned off. (Note that the warning chimes are never deactivated.)

Operation Keys

The operation keys enable you to adjust cooking times, change pressure levels, activate or cancel the Keep Warm and Delay Start modes, cancel any cooking program, or reset the pot to the original factory settings.

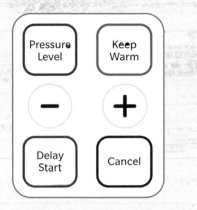

PRESSURE LEVEL: Adjusts the pressure level between high and low pressure, for whichever program has been selected.

KEEP WARM: Keeps food warm after the cooking process is complete, or when using the pot as a food warmer.

[–] BUTTON: Decreases the cook time, adjusts the Delay Start and Keep Warm times, and turns the sounds off. (Hold for three seconds to turn off sounds.)

[+] BUTTON: Decreases the cook time, adjusts the Delay Start and Keep Warm times, and turns on the sounds. (Hold for three seconds to turn sounds back on.)

DELAY: Delays the start of a cooking program by as little as 10 minutes, or up to 24 hours. Activate by selecting the desired cooking program, then selecting Delay Start.

CANCEL: Cancels a cooking program and returns the pot to standby mode, which is indicated by **OFF** on the LCD display. To reset the pot to the original factory settings, press and hold for approximately ten seconds, or until the pot emits a beep.

Cooking Program Keys

The cooking program keys enable you to choose from a variety of preprogrammed settings on the Instant Pot. Each program has default time and temperature settings designed to cook specific types of foods, but each can be adjusted using the operation keys.

PRESSURE COOK: Also listed as **Manual** on some Instant Pot models, this is the setting you're likely to use the most. The temperature mode, pressure levels, and cooking times can all be controlled through the operation keys on the control panel.

MEAT/STEW: Best for cooking large cuts of meat at high pressure. For a softer meat texture, use the **Less** mode; for a very tender meat texture, use the **Normal** mode; for a texture that is fall-off-the-bone tender, use the **More** mode.

BEAN/CHILI: Using this high pressure program results in different doneness levels for beans. For a firmer bean texture, use the **Less** mode; for a softer bean texture, use the **Normal** mode; for a very soft bean texture, use the **More** mode.

CAKE: This high pressure mode creates a very moist, dense cake. For a lighter, moister cake, use the **Less** mode; for a denser cake, use the **Normal** mode; for a really dense cake, such as a cheesecake, use the **More** mode.

EGG: This program is designed for cooking extra-large eggs, so you may need to adjust the mode for smaller eggs. For a soft-cooked egg, use the **Less** mode; for a medium-cooked egg, use the **Normal** mode; for a hard-cooked egg, use the **More** mode.

SLOW COOK: Use the **Less** mode to correspond to a low (8 hour) slow cooker setting; use the **Normal** mode to correspond to a medium (6 hour) slow cooker setting; use the **More** mode to correspond to a high (4 hour) slow cooker setting.

SAUTÉ: You can sauté food in your Instant Pot just as you would in a pan, using just a small amount of oil. Use **Less** mode for simmering and for foods that may burn easily; use **Normal** mode for searing; use **More** mode for browning and stir frying.

RICE: This program cooks on low pressure, and is best used for white rice. For rice with a firmer texture, use the **Less** mode; for rice with a normal texture, use the **Normal** mode; for rice with a softer texture, use the **More** mode.

MULTIGRAIN: Includes a presoaking time, and is best for brown rice, wild rice, and tougher whole grains. For a firmer texture, use the **Less** mode; for a normal texture, use the **Normal** mode; for a softer texture, use the **More** mode.

PORRIDGE: Cooks at high pressure, and is used for making white rice porridge (congee). Use the **Less** or **Normal** modes for making a simple rice porridge; use the **More** mode for a porridge that contains beans or tougher grains.

STEAM: For steaming vegetables, use the **Less** mode; for seafood and fish, use the **Normal** mode; for meats, use the **More** mode. (Always use the quick release method to prevent overcooking the food, and always use the steam rack.)

STERILIZE: This program is designed for canning. Use the **Less** mode to pasteurize dairy products; use the **Normal** mode for low pressure sterilization and canning; use the **More** mode for high pressure sterilization and canning.

YOGURT: The **Normal** mode is used for fermenting milk, while the **More** mode is used for pasteurizing milk. (The **Less** mode is designed to make Jiu Niang, a sweet fermented rice dish popular in Chinese cuisine.)

SOUP/BROTH: Brings soups to a slow simmer, and also results in a clear broth. For meatless soups, use the **Less** mode; for soups with meats, use the **Normal** mode; for soups that require longer cook times, such as bone broths, use the **More** mode.

Getting to Know Your Instant Pot®

Because the Instant Pot has a variety of different functions and programs, it looks and works a little differently than other appliances you may already own. These are some of the features you'll find on the Instant Pot, as well as some of the accessories that are essential to own.

BASE AND LID
The base and lid are the brains and bones of your Instant Pot. The base holds the inner pot and houses the controls, and the lid seals the pot. The outer surfaces need only to be wiped down with a damp cloth between uses. The interiors should be wiped down only when the pot is cool.

LOCKING PIN
The locking pin mechanism is located on the lid and serves as a catch mechanism for keeping the lid safe and secure on the base. When the lid is secured over the pot, the pin will be recessed.

CONDENSATION COLLECTOR CUP
The condensation collector cup collects any excess moisture that leaks from the Instant Pot during the cooking process, helping prevent unnecessary messes. The condensation collector cup should be drained, rinsed, and washed in hot, soapy water after each use.

STEAM RELEASE HANDLE
The steam release handle (also called the steam release valve) is the switch that is toggled back and forth to seal the Instant Pot for cooking. When the handle is toggled to the closed position (**Sealing**), the pot will be able to build and maintain pressure. When the handle is toggled to the open position (**Venting**), the pot will release steam through the vent on the top of the handle. The position of the handle will depend on which cooking program has been selected.

FLOAT VALVE
The float valve indicates if the cooking chamber has been pressurized. If the float valve is in the up position, the pot contains pressure that needs to be released before you can open the lid. If the float valve is in the down position, the pot is not pressurized. Always make sure the float valve is down before attempting to open the lid on your pot.

SEALING INDICATOR

The sealing indicator is simply a series of markings on the lid and base that help identify when the lid is closed or open. The indicator features arrows that, when properly aligned, will show the sealing positions of the lid and base.

HANDLES

The handles enable you to hold and transport the pot safely, and also serve as handy lid holders to keep the lid off the countertop to help minimize messes.

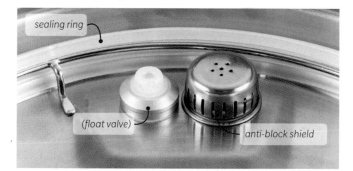

sealing ring

(float valve)

anti-block shield

SEALING RING

The sealing ring creates the essential seal for pressure cooking. If it's not seated properly, is dirty, or is damaged, the Instant Pot may not seal properly. It should be washed in hot, soapy water after every use.

ANTI-BLOCK SHIELD

The anti-block shield covers the interior side of the steam release handle and prevents the valve from becoming clogged. It should be removed and washed in hot, soapy water after every use.

Accessories

Here are a few important accessories to have on hand when you're cooking with your Instant Pot.

INNER POT

The stainless steel inner pot is included with the Instant Pot and is the vessel that holds the food being cooked. It rests inside the base and can be removed for easy cleanup with hot, soapy water.

STEAM RACK

The steam rack also is included with the Instant Pot and can be used for holding items that need to be steamed, or for holding oddly shaped foods that need to be elevated out of cooking liquids.

TEMPERED GLASS LID

The tempered glass lid is an optional accessory that is not included with the Instant Pot, but it's essential to own. The lid fits over the inner pot and can be used for several cooking programs that do not require pressure, such as slow cooking or sautéing. Tempered glass lids can be purchased online.

Using Your Instant Pot®

Mastering the Instant Pot can take some practice and a bit of know-how, but understanding these concepts will help shorten the learning curve as you're familiarizing yourself with this amazing appliance.

SEALING

Proper sealing is critical to achieving the expected results in the Instant Pot. The lid will only lock into place if the sealing ring is properly seated inside the lid. If the lid isn't seated properly, an error message will be displayed on the LCD display. If you remove the lid to add an ingredient, and then attempt to close and lock the lid back in place when there's still hot food in the inner pot, the pressure may still be too high and the pot may not seal. If this occurs, simply wait a few minutes for the contents to cool down a bit and then replace the lid. Once the lid is properly seated, the Instant Pot will indicate proper sealing through a brief rising chime. If the sealing is successful, the pot will initiate the selected program and no longer show an error code.

ATMOSPHERIC PRESSURE

Because you're cooking with pressure, atmospheric pressure can have an impact on total cooking times. For locations below an elevation of 2,000 feet above sea level, no additional adjustments are necessary; however, for locations at or above 2,000 feet, you should increase the cooking times by 5 percent for every 1,000 feet at or above the 2,000-foot sea level.

VOLUME

As a general rule, the more volume you have in the pot, the longer it will take for the pot to reach full pressurization, and the longer it will take for the pressure to naturally release once the cooking time is complete. For consistent results, always stay at or below the markings on the inner pot when adding food to the inner pot. For pressure cooking, you should never fill the inner pot past the **PC Max—2/3** indicator stamped on the inside of the inner pot. For many foods, it's best to keep the volume at or below the **1/2** mark that is stamped on the inner pot, particularly for foods that tend to expand in volume during cooking, such as beans or pasta.

TEMPERATURE

The temperature of foods that you place in the Instant Pot can have a direct impact on results. Placing cold or frozen foods in the Instant Pot can directly impact how long it takes for the pot to achieve full pressurization and temperature. You should always consider this when planning your cooking times, and assume that the colder the foods are that you are placing in the pot, the longer the build times will be. Room temperature can also have some impact on build and cooking times.

Pressure Release Methods

QUICK PRESSURE RELEASE

Quick pressure release is achieved by manually flipping the steam release handle to the venting position. Quick pressure release is useful for vegetables, pasta, and other foods that can quickly become overcooked and mushy. Note that the quick release method should be done with caution, as the pot releases the pressure rapidly and can cause burns, so never place your hand or face directly over the vent on the steam release handle. Always toggle the handle from the side. (As an added precaution, you can use a wooden spoon to flip the handle to the venting position.)

NATURAL PRESSURE RELEASE

Natural pressure release is initiated automatically by the Instant Pot when a pressure cooking program is completed, or when the **Cancel** button is pressed. Stews, whole grains, and meat dishes typically benefit from the additional cooking time a natural release allows because the additional time helps tenderize tougher foods. Natural pressure release can take significantly longer than quick pressure release—typically anywhere between 5 to 30 minutes, depending on what is being cooked, the pressure at which it is being cooked, and the volume of food in the pot.

Cooking Times

Each recipe in this book includes a total time, which factors in four different time components: prep time, build time, cook time, and release time. Understanding how these times work, and how they can impact the total time in a recipe, will help you plan your time in the kichen accordingly.

PREP TIME

The prep time is the approximate amount of time it will take to prepare any of the ingredients for cooking in the Instant Pot. This may include chopping and slicing raw ingredients, such as vegetables, or precooking other ingredients for use in the main recipe. What is not included in the prep time are any preparations that take place in the Instant Pot, or any cooking processes that take place outside of the pot, such as broiling, baking, or stovetop cooking methods.

BUILD TIME

The build time is the time is takes for the Instant Pot to get up to full pressure, once the program has been selected and the lid has been closed. How long this takes can depend on a number of factors including the total volume of food in the pot, the temperature of food, atmospheric pressure, and room temperature. The build time can vary significantly based on these factors, but as a general rule the recipes in this book factor in a 10–20 minute total build time for most recipes.

COOK TIME

The cook time includes only the actual amount of time the food is being cooked in the Instant Pot in the period between full pressurization and the time pressure release has been completed. The cook time also will include other methods in a recipe, such as sautéing, baking, or broiling. The cook time does not include build times, it includes only the actual time the food is being cooked.

RELEASE TIME

The release time in a recipe can vary significantly, based on the method called for in the recipe. Natural release can add a significant amount of time to the total recipe time—in many instances between 5–30 minutes. The estimated natural release time is included in the recipe instructions. Quick release times are significantly shorter, and will range between 30 seconds and 2 minutes.

Other Helpful Tips

ACHIEVING CRISPY TEXTURES

One challenge with pressure cooking is achieving crispy textures, since the moist heat of pressure cooking doesn't create crispy-finished foods. The **Sauté** function on the Instant Pot can help further develop flavors and add crust. When sautéing foods in the Instant Pot, you can adjust the level of heat between **Low**, **Normal**, and **More**. The recipes in this book were created using the **Normal** setting, but the **More** setting can be useful when trying to boil down a sauce, and the **Low** setting is useful when cooking foods that can easily burn.

COOKING WITH ALCOHOL

A few recipes in this book use a modest amount of alcohol. Pressure cooking temperatures are high enough to deplete alcohol, but since pressure cooking occurs in a sealed environment, some alcohol may still remain.

MAKING DOUBLE BATCHES

Many recipes in this book can be doubled for making larger batches. When doubling recipes, it's critical to never fill the inner pot past the markings on the inside of the pot. This will ensure that there will be ample room for foods like beans to expand, once the pressure builds.

MAKING SUBSTITUTIONS

Some recipes in this book utilize other recipes in the book as ingredients. Store-bought versions of these ingredients may be substituted, but always look for options that are comparable in nutrition to the recipe in the book. In addition, some recipes may call for a vegetable oil spread to add a buttery flavor to recipes, and is used when deemed to be a better option than butter. Always look for a spread such as Smart Balance that is high in Omega-3 fats, and low in trans fats.

Breakfast

Maple Brown Sugar Oatmeal

Kids will love this hearty, satisfying breakfast classic that is ready in 15 minutes in the Instant Pot. It's way better than anything you'll get from a package.

PROGRAM
Pressure Cook

PRESSURE
High

RELEASE
Quick

1 cup rolled oats

1¾ cups water

Pinch kosher salt

1 tbsp maple syrup

2 tsp light brown sugar, lightly packed

1 medium banana, sliced

1. Spray the inner pot with nonstick cooking spray. Combine the oats, water, and kosher salt in the pot. Stir to combine.

2. Cover, lock the lid, and flip the steam release handle to the sealing position. Select **Pressure Cook (High)**, and set the cook time for **4 minutes**. When the cook time is complete, quick release the pressure.

3. Remove the lid. Add the maple syrup and brown sugar. Stir to combine.

4. Transfer to serving bowls and top each serving with half of the sliced banana. Serve warm.

NUTRITION PER SERVING

Total fat **244g**	Cholesterol **72mg**	Carbohydrates **51g**	Sugars **19g**
Saturated fat **1g**	Sodium **72mg**	Dietary fiber **6g**	Protein **6g**

Ham and Cheddar Frittata

This protein-packed egg dish can be served for any meal of the day. Whole eggs add an extra nutritional punch with liver-boosting choline and antioxidants.

289 CALORIES PER SERVING

SERVES **2**
SERVING SIZE **2 cups**
PREP TIME **5 mins**
COOK TIME **20 mins**
TOTAL TIME **35 mins**

 PROGRAM
Pressure Cook

 PRESSURE
Low

RELEASE
Quick

1. Place the steam rack in the inner pot, and add 1 cup water to the bottom of the pot. Spray a 1-quart (1l) soufflé dish with nonstick cooking spray, and lightly wipe the interior of the dish with a paper towel to remove any excess spray.

2. Combine the eggs, milk, kosher salt, and pepper in a large bowl. Whisk to combine.

3. Add the ham, bell pepper, and ¼ cup of the cheese to the bowl. Stir gently to combine.

4. Pour the egg mixture into the prepared soufflé dish, and sprinkle the remaining cheese over top. Loosely cover the dish with aluminum foil, and carefully lower onto the steam rack.

5. Cover, lock the lid, and flip the steam release handle to the sealing position. Select **Pressure Cook (Low)**, and set the cook time for **20 minutes**. When the cook time is complete, quick release the pressure.

6. Carefully transfer the soufflé dish to a cooling rack and allow the frittata to cool for at least 5 minutes before slicing. Serve warm.

4 large eggs
2 tbsp low-fat milk
½ tsp kosher salt
¼ tsp freshly ground black pepper
2oz (55g) lean deli ham, chopped
¼ cup finely diced bell pepper
½ cup shredded cheddar cheese, divided

Cooking eggs on low pressure helps prevent them from becoming tough.

NUTRITION PER SERVING

Total fat **19g**	Cholesterol **420mg**	Carbohydrates **3g**	Sugars **2g**
Saturated fat **8g**	Sodium **546mg**	Dietary fiber **0g**	Protein **25g**

311 CALORIES
PER SERVING

SERVES **4**
SERVING SIZE **1 slice**
PREP TIME **10 mins**
COOK TIME **30 mins**
TOTAL TIME **55 mins**

Peach French Toast Casserole

This naturally sweetened breakfast casserole is loaded with protein and whole grains. It's a great way to turn that day-old bread into a delicious breakfast!

  PROGRAM
Pressure Cook

  PRESSURE
Low

RELEASE
Quick

4 tsp unsalted butter, divided
6 slices whole grain bread, cut into ½-inch (1.25cm) cubes (about 4 cups)
2 large eggs
1 cup whole milk
½ tsp ground cinnamon
¾ cup packed-in-juice canned peaches
2 tbsp chopped pecans
1 tsp confectioners' sugar
4 tbsp maple syrup

1. Place the steam rack in the inner pot, and add 1 cup water to the bottom of the pot.

2. Coat the interior of a 1-quart (1l) soufflé dish with 1 teaspoon of the butter, and then add the bread cubes to the dish.

3. In a medium bowl, combine the eggs, milk, and cinnamon. Whisk to combine, and then add the peaches and canning juice. Stir to combine.

4. Pour the egg mixture over the bread cubes, and gently press the cubes into egg mixture until thoroughly coated in the mixture.

5. Cut the remaining butter into small pieces and evenly distribute over top of the bread cubes. Loosely cover the soufflé dish with aluminum foil.

6. Cover, lock the lid, and flip the steam release handle to the sealing position. Select **Pressure Cook (Low)**, and set the cook time for **30 minutes**. When the cook time is complete, quick release the pressure.

7. Remove the lid. Carefully transfer the dish to a cooling rack, and allow the casserole to cool for 10 minutes.

8. Garnish with the pecans and dust with the confectioners' sugar. Cut into 4 equal-sized portions, and drizzle 1 tablespoon maple syrup over top of each portion just before serving. Serve warm.

This recipe can be made the night before and baked right before breakfast!

NUTRITION PER SERVING

Total fat **11g**	Cholesterol **106mg**	Carbohydrates **42g**	Sugars **28g**
Saturated fat **4g**	Sodium **299mg**	Dietary fiber **4g**	Protein **11g**

175 CALORIES
PER SERVING

SERVES **4**
SERVING SIZE **1 cup**
PREP TIME **2 mins**
COOK TIME **10 mins**
TOTAL TIME **17 mins**

20-Minute Steel Cut Oats

With 4 grams of hunger-fighting fiber and 7 grams of protein per serving, these delicious and satisfying oats will keep you feeling full all morning long.

 PROGRAM
Pressure Cook

PRESSURE
High

RELEASE
Quick

1 cup steel cut oats
2½ cups water
½ tsp ground cinnamon
1 tbsp light brown sugar
¼ tsp kosher salt
1 cup fresh strawberries, sliced

1. Spray the inner pot with nonstick cooking spray. Combine the oats, water, cinnamon, brown sugar, and kosher salt in the pot. Stir well.

2. Cover, lock the lid, and flip the steam release handle to the sealing position. Select **Pressure Cook (High)**, and set the cook time for **10 minutes**. When the cook time is complete, quick release the pressure.

3. Remove the lid, and allow the oats to cool slightly in the pot. Transfer to serving bowls and garnish each serving with ¼ cup of the strawberry slices. Serve warm.

A less processed form of oats, these high-fiber grains have a pleasantly chewy texture.

NUTRITION PER SERVING

Total fat **3g**	Cholesterol **0mg**	Carbohydrates **30g**	Sugars **3g**
Saturated fat **0g**	Sodium **155mg**	Dietary fiber **4g**	Protein **7g**

Pumpkin Pie Oatmeal

This recipe features all the flavors of pumpkin pie rolled into a cozy, healthy breakfast. Pumpkin adds fiber and vitamins, and will help keep you energized.

272 CALORIES PER SERVING

SERVES **2**
SERVING SIZE **1 cup**
PREP TIME **2 mins**
COOK TIME **4 mins**
TOTAL TIME **15 mins**

 PROGRAM
Pressure Cook

 PRESSURE
High

RELEASE
Quick

1. Divide the pumpkin seeds and crushed animal crackers into 4 equal-sized portions. Set aside.

2. Spray the inner pot with nonstick cooking spray. Combine the oats, Pumpkin-Apple Butter, water, and kosher salt in the inner pot. Stir well.

3. Cover, lock the lid, and flip the steam release handle to the sealing position. Select **Pressure Cook (High),** and set the cook time for **4 minutes**. When the cook time is complete, quick release the pressure.

4. Remove the lid, and stir. Transfer to serving bowls, and top each serving with the pumpkin seed and animal cracker mix. Serve warm.

1 tbsp pumpkin seeds
½ cup crushed animal crackers
1 cup rolled oats
¼ cup **Pumpkin-Apple Butter (see p30)**
1½ cups water
Pinch kosher salt

NUTRITION PER SERVING

Total fat **5g**	Cholesterol **0mg**	Carbohydrates **54g**	Sugars **17g**
Saturated fat **1g**	Sodium **124mg**	Dietary fiber **9g**	Protein **7g**

Spinach and Sun-Dried Tomato Oatmeal

226 CALORIES
PER SERVING

SERVES **2**
SERVING SIZE **1 cup**
PREP TIME **10 mins**
COOK TIME **10 mins**
TOTAL TIME **25 mins**

Savory oats for breakfast? Absolutely! Start your day off right with this bowl of high-protein goodness that contains 20% of your daily needs for fiber.

 PROGRAM
Pressure Cook

 PRESSURE
High

 RELEASE
Quick

2 tbsp white vinegar
2 large eggs
1 cup uncooked rolled oats
1¾ cups water
Pinch kosher salt
1 cup fresh baby spinach
1 tbsp grated Parmesan cheese
2 tbsp packed-in-oil
 sun-dried tomatoes,
 drained and chopped

1. Fill a medium saucepan with cold water, and add the vinegar. Bring to a simmer over low heat.

2. Working one at a time, crack an egg into a small bowl, swirl the water in the pan, and then immediately pour the egg into the water. Poach for 3 minutes, and then use a slotted spoon to transfer the egg to a plate lined with a paper towel. Repeat with the remaining egg. Set aside.

3. Spray the inner pot with nonstick cooking spray. Combine the oats, water, and kosher salt in the pot. Stir well.

4. Cover, lock the lid, and flip the steam release handle to the sealing position. Select **Pressure Cook (High)**, and set the cook time for **4 minutes**. When the cook time is complete, quick release the pressure.

5. Remove the lid. Add the spinach and Parmesan. Mix well.

6. Transfer to serving bowls and top each serving with 1 tablespoon of the sun-dried tomatoes and 1 egg. Serve warm.

NUTRITION PER SERVING

Total fat **7g**	Cholesterol **97mg**	Carbohydrates **30g**	Sugars **1g**
Saturated fat **2g**	Sodium **205mg**	Dietary fiber **5g**	Protein **11g**

SERVES **2**
SERVING SIZE **1 slice**
PREP TIME **10 mins**
COOK TIME **25 mins**
TOTAL TIME **40 mins**

Bagel and Egg Breakfast Casserole

High in protein and big on flavor, and with the perfect amount of cheese and a bite of bagel (yes, bagel!), this hearty breakfast casserole will satisfy big cravings.

 PROGRAM
Pressure Cook

PRESSURE
Low

RELEASE
Quick

1 small sweet potato

4 large eggs

2 tbsp low-fat milk

½ tsp kosher salt

¼ tsp freshly ground black pepper

½ toasted bagel (preferably whole-grain), cut into bite-sized pieces

¼ cup chopped fresh broccoli florets

½ cup low-fat shredded pepper jack cheese, divided

1. Using a fork, pierce the sweet potato a few times, and then place it in the microwave to cook on high for 5 minutes, or until it's just fork tender. Allow to cool, and then remove the skin and dice.

2. Place the steam rack in the inner pot and add 1 cup of water to the bottom of the pot. Spray a 1-quart (1l) soufflé dish with nonstick cooking spray, and use a clean paper towel to lightly wipe away any excess cooking spray from the inside of the dish.

3. In a large bowl, combine the eggs, milk, kosher salt, and pepper. Whisk to combine. Add the bagel pieces, sweet potato, broccoli, and ¼ cup of the cheese to the bowl. Stir gently.

4. Pour the egg mixture into the prepared the soufflé dish, and sprinkle the remaining cheese over top. Carefully lower the dish into the pot and loosely cover the dish with aluminum foil.

5. Cover, lock the lid, and flip the steam release handle to the sealing position. Select **Pressure Cook (Low)**, and set the cook time for **20 minutes**. When the cook time is complete, quick release the pressure.

6. Carefully remove the dish from the pot and allow the casserole to cool for 5 minutes before slicing. Serve warm.

Assemble this casserole the night before and toss it in the Instant Pot in the morning!

NUTRITION PER SERVING

Total fat **16g**	Cholesterol **393mg**	Carbohydrates **24g**	Sugars **3g**
Saturated fat **6g**	Sodium **506mg**	Dietary fiber **3g**	Protein **25g**

Coconut Matcha Quinoa

This unique porridge features creamy, coconut-simmered quinoa and a flavor boost from inflammation-fighting, cell-protecting green tea matcha powder.

435 CALORIES PER SERVING

SERVES **4**
SERVING SIZE **1 cup**
PREP TIME **5 mins**
COOK TIME **15 mins**
TOTAL TIME **25 mins**

PROGRAM
Pressure Cook

PRESSURE
High

RELEASE
Natural

1. Spray the inner pot with nonstick cooking spray. Combine the dried cranberries and pumpkin seeds in a small bowl. Set aside.

2. Combine the quinoa, coconut milk, water, matcha powder, honey, and salt in the inner pot. Stir well.

3. Cover, lock the lid, and flip the steam release handle to the sealing position. Select **Pressure Cook (High)**, and set the cook time for **5 minutes**. When the cook time is complete, allow the pressure to release naturally (about 10 minutes).

4. Remove the lid, stir, and then transfer to serving bowls. Top each serving with 1 tablespoon of the cranberry and pumpkin seed mixture. Serve warm.

2 tbsp dried cranberries
2 tbsp roasted pumpkin seeds
1 cup quinoa (white or red), rinsed and drained
½ cup coconut milk
½ cup water
1 tsp green tea matcha powder
1 tbsp honey
Pinch salt

NUTRITION PER SERVING

Total fat **10g**	Cholesterol **0mg**	Carbohydrates **36g**	Sugars **7g**
Saturated fat **6g**	Sodium **42mg**	Dietary fiber **3g**	Protein **7g**

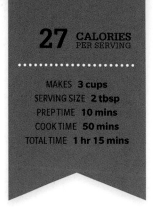

27 CALORIES
PER SERVING

MAKES **3 cups**
SERVING SIZE **2 tbsp**
PREP TIME **10 mins**
COOK TIME **50 mins**
TOTAL TIME **1 hr 15 mins**

Pumpkin-Apple Butter

This velvety, caramelized sauce is low in sugar, fat-free, and delicious slathered on toast, added to a smoothie, or used as a fat substitute in baked goods.

PROGRAM
Pressure Cook/Sauté

PRESSURE
High

RELEASE
Natural

3lbs (1.4kg) apples (Gala, Fuji, or McIntosh varieties), peeled, cored, and roughly chopped
15oz (420g) can pumpkin purée
½ cup water
1 tsp ground cinnamon
½ tsp ground ginger

1. Combine the apples, pumpkin purée, and water in the inner pot. Stir well.

2. Cover, lock the lid, and flip the steam release handle to the sealing position. Select **Pressure Cook (High)**, and set the cook time for **10 minutes**. When the cook time is complete, allow the pressure to release naturally (about 15 minutes).

3. Remove the lid, and add the cinnamon and ginger. Using an immersion blender, purée the ingredients until a smooth consistency is achieved, and no lumps remain.

4. Select **Sauté** and cook the butter for an additional 25 minutes, stirring frequently, until the mixture thickens, develops a dark brown color, and begins to caramelize. Select **Cancel** to turn off the heat, and allow the butter to cool slightly in the pot.

5. Ladle into sealable glass jars and allow to cool completely before sealing. Store in the refrigerator for up to 2 weeks.

For a different flavor, substitute cardamom, nutmeg, or ground cloves for the cinnamon.

NUTRITION PER SERVING

Total fat **0g**	Cholesterol **0mg**	Carbohydrates **9g**	Sugars **7g**
Saturated fat **0g**	Sodium **1mg**	Dietary fiber **2g**	Protein **0g**

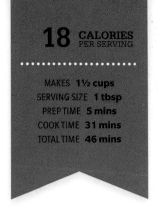

18 CALORIES
PER SERVING

MAKES **1½ cups**
SERVING SIZE **1 tbsp**
PREP TIME **5 mins**
COOK TIME **31 mins**
TOTAL TIME **46 mins**

Low-Sugar Pineapple Jam

This sweet and tangy jam has a third of the sugar found in most jams. It's lovely slathered on warm biscuits, mixed into yogurt, or used in salad dressings or marinades.

PROGRAM
Pressure Cook

PRESSURE
High

RELEASE
Natural

4 cups diced fresh pineapple
¼ cup evaporated cane sugar
Juice of 1 lime

1. Combine the pineapple, sugar, and lime juice in the inner pot. Stir gently.

2. Cover, lock the lid, and flip the steam release handle to the sealing position. Select **Pressure Cook (High)**, and set the cook time for **1 minute**. When the cook time is complete, allow the pressure to release naturally (about 15 minutes).

3. Remove the lid and stir. (If a smoother jam is desired, use an immersion blender to blend the ingredients until a smooth texture is achieved. If a thicker consistency is desired, select **Sauté** and simmer until the jam thickens [about 10 minutes], and then select **Cancel** to turn off the heat.)

4. Transfer to a large, sealable glass jar and allow to cool completely before sealing. Store in the refrigerator for up to 1 week.

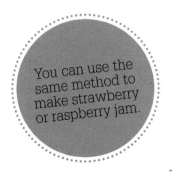

You can use the same method to make strawberry or raspberry jam.

NUTRITION PER SERVING

Total fat **0g**	Cholesterol **0mg**	Carbohydrates **5g**	Sugars **4g**
Saturated fat **0g**	Sodium **0mg**	Dietary fiber **0g**	Protein **0g**

Homemade Greek Yogurt

This smooth and creamy yogurt is versatile and worth the effort. Serve it with fruit and granola, or whisk it into soups, sauces, or desserts. One taste and you'll be hooked!

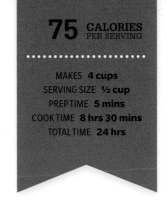

75 CALORIES
PER SERVING

MAKES **4 cups**
SERVING SIZE **½ cup**
PREP TIME **5 mins**
COOK TIME **8 hrs 30 mins**
TOTAL TIME **24 hrs**

 PROGRAM
Yogurt

 PRESSURE
none

RELEASE
none

1. Add the milk to the inner pot. Cover and lock the lid, but leave the steam release handle in the venting position.

2. Select **Yogurt (Boil)**. Once the boil cycle is complete (about 30 minutes), carefully remove the inner pot from the base.

3. Fill a large, heat-resistant bowl halfway with ice water. Place the inner pot, with the milk, in the ice water bath. Chill the milk until it reaches a temperature of 115°F (46°C).

4. Once the milk has reached the target temperature, whisk in the Greek yogurt. Remove the inner pot from the ice water, dry the outside of the pot with a paper towel, and return it to the base.

5. Cover, lock the lid, but leave the steam release handle in the venting position. Once again select **Yogurt**, and set the cook time for **8 hours**. When the cook time is complete, carefully remove the lid and transfer the yogurt to a sealable container. Place the milk in the refrigerator to chill for a minimum of 8 hours.

6. Once the chilling time is complete, line a fine mesh sieve with a layer of cheesecloth, place the sieve over a large bowl, and pour the chilled yogurt into the sieve. Loosely cover the bowl and sieve with plastic wrap, and transfer to the refrigerator to strain for 6–8 hours. (The longer the yogurt is strained, the thicker it will become.)

7. Once the yogurt has reached the desired consistency, remove from the refrigerator and pour off the liquid. Serve immediately, or store in the refrigerator for up to 5 days, or freeze for up to 1 month.

5 cups whole milk
2 tbsp 2% plain Greek yogurt

Freeze leftover yogurt in ice cube trays for tossing into smoothies.

NUTRITION PER SERVING

Total fat **2g**	Cholesterol **8mg**	Carbohydrates **5g**	Sugars **5g**
Saturated fat **2g**	Sodium **38mg**	Dietary fiber **0g**	Protein **10g**

Breakfast Sorghum Bowl

Start your day feeling energized with this high-protein, antioxidant-filled breakfast bowl. Sorghum is a versatile, gluten-free grain that can be served at any meal.

324 CALORIES PER SERVING

SERVES **4**
SERVING SIZE **1**
PREP TIME **10 mins**
COOK TIME **20 mins**
TOTAL TIME **35 mins**

PROGRAM
Multigrain

PRESSURE
High

RELEASE
Quick

1. Combine the sorghum, kosher salt, and water in the inner pot. Stir well.

2. Cover, lock the lid, and flip the steam release handle to the sealing position. Select **Multigrain (High)** until the mode is set to **Less.**

3. While the sorghum is cooking, fill a medium saucepan with cold water, and add the vinegar. Bring to a simmer over low heat.

4. Working one at a time, crack an egg into a small bowl, swirl the water in the pan, and immediately pour the egg into the water. Poach the egg for 3 minutes, and then use a slotted spoon to transfer the egg to a plate lined with a paper towel. Repeat with the remaining eggs. Set aside.

5. When the cook time for the sorghum is complete (about 20 minutes), quick release the pressure, remove the lid, and transfer the sorghum to a large colander. Rinse under cold water and allow to drain completely.

6. Transfer to serving bowls and top each serving with a poached egg, ¼ of the sliced avocado, and 2 tablespoons of the salsa, and then season with the pepper. Serve warm.

1 cup pearled sorghum, rinsed and drained
½ tsp kosher salt
1½ cups water
1 tbsp white vinegar
4 large eggs
1 avocado, sliced
½ cup salsa
Freshly ground black pepper

NUTRITION PER SERVING

Total fat **12g**	Cholesterol **186mg**	Carbohydrates **43g**	Sugars **3g**
Saturated fat **2g**	Sodium **346mg**	Dietary fiber **7g**	Protein **13g**

Multigrain Hot Breakfast Cereal

250 CALORIES PER SERVING

SERVES **4**
SERVING SIZE **1 cup**
PREP TIME **10 mins**
COOK TIME **25 mins**
TOTAL TIME **40 mins**

This gluten-free cereal is loaded with whole grains and contains more protein, fiber, vitamins, minerals, and antioxidants than store-bought cereals.

 PROGRAM
Pressure Cook

 PRESSURE
High

 RELEASE
Natural/Quick

¼ cup long-grain brown rice
¼ cup quinoa (white or red)
¼ cup whole-grain sorghum
¼ cup rolled oats
6 tbsp sliced almonds, divided
2½ cups water
2 tbsp honey
½ cup low-fat milk
¼ cup **Homemade Greek Yogurt (see p33)** or low-fat Greek yogurt
¼ cup pomegranate arils

1. Make the multigrain flour by combining the brown rice, quinoa, sorghum, oats, and 4 tablespoons of the almonds in a blender or food processor. Grind the ingredients until a fine, flour-like consistency is achieved.

2. Transfer the multigrain flour to the inner pot, and then add the water and honey. Mix well to combine.

3. Cover, lock the lid, and flip the steam release handle to the sealing position. Select **Pressure Cook (High)**, and set the cook time for **15 minutes**. When the cook time is complete, allow the pressure to release naturally for 10 minutes, and then quick release the remaining pressure.

4. Remove the lid and stir in the milk. (If a thinner consistency is desired, add more water, 1 tbsp at a time, and stir until the desired consistency is achieved.)

5. Transfer to serving bowls, and top each serving with 1 tablespoon of the Greek yogurt, 1 tablespoon pomegranate arils, and 1½ teaspoons of the almonds. Serve hot.

NUTRITION PER SERVING

Total fat **6g**	Cholesterol **1mg**	Carbohydrates **43g**	Sugars **15g**
Saturated fat **1g**	Sodium **101mg**	Dietary fiber **5g**	Protein **12g**

Egg and Bacon Breakfast Sandwiches

I have fond memories of eating drive-thru breakfast sandwiches on family vacations. Here's a healthier version that's lower in fat, and also includes a serving of greens.

236 CALORIES PER SERVING

MAKES **3**
SERVING SIZE **1**
PREP TIME **5 mins**
COOK TIME **6 mins**
TOTAL TIME **21 mins**

 PROGRAM
Pressure Cook

 PRESSURE
High

 RELEASE
Quick

3 large eggs
¼ tsp kosher salt
Freshly ground black pepper
3 x .75oz (21g) slices Canadian bacon
3 tbsp shredded cheddar cheese
1 cup fresh baby spinach
3 whole wheat English muffins, sliced and toasted

1. Place the steam rack in the inner pot, and add 1 cup of water to the bottom of the pot. Spray 3 small ramekins with nonstick cooking spray, and crack 1 egg into each ramekin.

2. Transfer the ramekins to the pot. Season each with salt and pepper, and top with a slice of the Canadian bacon. Loosely cover the ramekins with aluminum foil.

3. Cover, lock the lid, and flip the steam release handle to the sealing position. Select **Pressure Cook (High)**, and set the cook time for **6 minutes**. When the cook time is complete, quick release the pressure.

4. Remove the lid and discard the foil. Using tongs, carefully transfer the ramekins to a cooling rack, and top each with 1 tablespoon of the cheese and ⅓ cup of the spinach. Allow to cool for 5 minutes.

5. Once cooled, turn each ramekin out onto an English muffin. Serve hot.

NUTRITION PER SERVING

Total fat **7g**	Cholesterol **196mg**	Carbohydrates **25g**	Sugars **2g**
Saturated fat **2g**	Sodium **499mg**	Dietary fiber **3g**	Protein **18g**

Blackberry Soy Milk Yogurt

While commercially prepared yogurts are often filled with processed ingredients, this delicious dairy-free breakfast contains only simple ingredients.

 PROGRAM
Yogurt

PRESSURE
none

RELEASE
none

4 cups plain, unsweetened soy milk

3 tbsp plain, dairy-free yogurt (soy, cashew, or almond)

2 tsp vanilla extract

1 pint fresh blackberries

2 tbsp roughly chopped pistachios

4 tbsp honey

1. Add the soy milk and yogurt to the inner pot. Stir well.

2. Cover and lock the lid, but leave the steam release handle in the venting position. Select **Yogurt**, and set the cook time for **14 hours**. When the cook time is complete, remove the lid and stir in the vanilla.

3. Allow the yogurt to cool slightly, and then transfer to a large, sealable glass jar, and seal tightly. Place in the refrigerator to chill and thicken for a minimum of 4 hours, or up to overnight.

4. To serve, transfer the chilled yogurt to serving bowls. Top each serving with ½ cup blackberries and 1½ teaspoons pistachios, and then drizzle 1 tablespoon honey over top. Store in the refrigerator for up to 5 days.

Use a clean-ingredient soy milk made with nothing but soybeans and water.

NUTRITION PER SERVING

Total fat **4g**	Cholesterol **0mg**	Carbohydrates **24g**	Sugars **17g**
Saturated fat **1g**	Sodium **93mg**	Dietary fiber **5g**	Protein **8g**

Dinner

235 CALORIES PER SERVING

SERVES **12**
SERVING SIZE **¾ cup**
PREP TIME **10 mins**
COOK TIME **1 hr 42 mins**
TOTAL TIME **2 hrs 10 mins**

Korean Barbecue Beef

Forget about high-fat meats and sugary sauces, this version has all the flavor of traditional Korean barbeque beef, but with less sugar and less fat.

PROGRAM
Sauté/Pressure Cook

PRESSURE
High

RELEASE
Natural

3 tbsp lightly packed light brown sugar

2 tsp ground ginger

¼ cup reduced-sodium soy sauce

1 tbsp Sambal Oelek hot chili paste

½ yellow onion, sliced

1 tbsp canola oil

4lbs (1.8kg) boneless chuck roast

1 tsp kosher salt

¾ cup water

1 cup fresh cilantro, chopped

lime wedges, for serving

1. Make the sauce by combining the brown sugar, ginger, soy sauce, Sambal Oelek, and onion in a medium bowl. Mix well, and set aside.

2. Select **Sauté**, and add the canola oil to the inner pot. Season the roast with the kosher salt.

3. Transfer the roast to the pot. Using tongs to turn the roast periodically, sauté until lightly browned on both sides, about 2–3 minutes. Once the roast is browned, add the sauce and water to the pot.

4. Cover, lock the lid, and flip the steam release handle to the sealing position. Select **Pressure Cook (High)**, and set the cook time for **1 hour 15 minutes**. When the cook time is complete, allow the pressure to release naturally (about 15 minutes).

5. Remove the lid, transfer the roast to a serving platter, and use forks to shred. Sprinkle the cilantro over top and serve with lime wedges on the side. Serve warm.

Reserve the leftover broth as a savory snack, or use as a base for soups.

NUTRITION PER SERVING

Total fat **10g**	Cholesterol **104mg**	Carbohydrates **4g**	Sugars **3g**
Saturated fat **4g**	Sodium **416mg**	Dietary fiber **0g**	Protein **32g**

Creamy Mushroom Risotto

There's nothing more comforting than a warm batch of risotto. This savory, vegetarian recipe can be made in less than 40 minutes, start to finish, in the Instant Pot.

297 CALORIES
PER SERVING

SERVES **6**
SERVING SIZE **1 cup**
PREP TIME **10 mins**
COOK TIME **25 mins**
TOTAL TIME **42 mins**
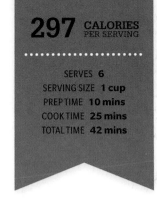

PROGRAM
Pressure Cook

PRESSURE
High

RELEASE
Natural/Quick

1. Select **Sauté**, and add the butter and onion to the inner pot. Sauté for 2–3 minutes, and then add the kosher salt and pepper.

2. Add the olive oil, mushrooms, and thyme to the pot. Sauté for an additional 2 minutes. Add the rice and stir well to coat with the oil.

3. Add the wine and cook until the liquid evaporates, stirring continuously. Stir in the chicken stock.

4. Cover, lock the lid, and flip the steam release handle to the sealing position. Select **Pressure Cook (High)**, and set the cook time for **10 minutes**. When the cook time is complete, allow the pressure to release naturally for 10 minutes, and then quick release the remaining pressure.

5. Remove the lid and stir in the Parmesan and parsley. Transfer to serving bowls. Serve hot.

1 tbsp unsalted butter

½ medium yellow onion, finely chopped

¾ tsp kosher salt

¼ tsp freshly ground black pepper

1 tbsp olive oil

8oz (225g) fresh baby portobello or crimini mushrooms, sliced

2 tsp chopped fresh thyme

1½ cups uncooked Arborio rice

2 tbsp dry white wine

3½ cups **From-Scratch Chicken Stock (see p100)** or low-sodium chicken stock

½ cup freshly grated Parmesan cheese

½ cup chopped fresh parsley

NUTRITION PER SERVING

Total fat **8g**	Cholesterol **12mg**	Carbohydrates **47g**	Sugars **2g**
Saturated fat **3g**	Sodium **318mg**	Dietary fiber **2g**	Protein **11g**

Pot Roast for A Crowd

It doesn't get more comforting than this one-pot classic!
Fork-tender beef and perfectly cooked vegetables make a
delicious meal, without a high-fat gravy or lots of wine.

266 CALORIES PER SERVING

SERVES **6**
SERVING SIZE **3½ oz (99g) +**
1½ oz (43g) vegetables
PREP TIME **10 mins**
COOK TIME **1 hr 20 mins**
TOTAL TIME **1 hr 45 mins**

PROGRAM **Sauté/Pressure Cook**	PRESSURE **High**	RELEASE **Natural**

1. Select **Sauté**, and add the olive oil to the inner pot. Season the roast with the kosher salt and pepper.

2. Transfer the roast to the pot and sauté until lightly browned, about 2–3 minutes per side, using tongs to turn the roast periodically. Transfer to a plate and set aside.

3. Add the onion, garlic, and thyme to the pot, and sauté for an additional 3 minutes. Add the beef broth and tomato paste. Using a wooden spoon, mix the ingredients well, and scrape any browned bits from the bottom of the pot.

4. Transfer the roast back to the pot. Add the carrots, potatoes, and bay leaf.

5. Cover, lock the lid, and flip the steam release handle to the sealing position. Select **Pressure Cook (High)**, and set the cook time for **50 minutes**. When the cook time is complete, allow the pressure to release naturally (about 20 minutes).

6. Remove the lid, discard the bay leaf, and transfer the roast and vegetables to a large serving platter. Serve warm.

1 tbsp olive oil
2lbs (1kg) boneless chuck roast
1 tsp kosher salt
½ tsp freshly ground
  black pepper
1 small yellow onion,
  thinly sliced
2 cloves garlic, finely chopped
1 tsp ground thyme
1½ cups beef broth
1 tbsp tomato paste
3 medium carrots, peeled
  and cut into large chunks
¾lb (340g) baby potatoes
1 bay leaf

NUTRITION PER SERVING

Total fat **293g**	Cholesterol **106mg**	Carbohydrates **14g**	Sugars **3g**
Saturated fat **12g**	Sodium **530mg**	Dietary fiber **2g**	Protein **33g**

Indoor Shrimp Boil

My family loves a shrimp boil, and the Instant Pot makes this hearty one-pot meal in a fraction of the time! Lean chicken sausage helps cut the fat and calories.

PROGRAM
Pressure Cook

PRESSURE
High

RELEASE
Quick

2 cups **From-Scratch Chicken Stock (see p100)** or low-sodium chicken stock

1 lemon, cut in half, with one half cut into wedges

1 lb (450g) baby Yukon gold potatoes

3 ears yellow corn, shucked and cut in half

2 heaping tsp Old Bay seasoning (or equivalent seafood seasoning)

½ tsp kosher salt

4 x 3oz (85g) links fully cooked Andouille chicken sausage, each cut into four pieces

1 lb (450g) large raw shrimp, peeled and deveined

4 tbsp butter, melted

1. Add the chicken stock to the inner pot, followed by one lemon half, the potatoes, and then the corn. Season with the Old Bay and kosher salt.

2. Add the sausage to the pot, followed by the shrimp.

3. Cover, lock the lid, and flip the steam release handle to the sealing position. Select **Pressure Cook (High)**, and set the cook time for **9 minutes**. When the cook time is complete, quick release the pressure.

4. Line a large sheet pan with parchment paper. Remove the lid and pour the boil out onto the pan. Serve with the melted butter and lemon wedges on the side. Serve hot.

NUTRITION PER SERVING

Total fat **16g**	Cholesterol **175mg**	Carbohydrates **30g**	Sugars **4g**
Saturated fat **8g**	Sodium **758mg**	Dietary fiber **4g**	Protein **30g**

Slow-Cooked Sweet and Spicy Pulled Chicken

This is the perfect set-it-and-forget-it meal for a busy weeknight. Add the ingredients to the Instant Pot in the morning for a healthy, flavorful dinner at night.

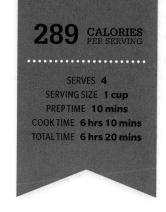

289 CALORIES PER SERVING

SERVES **4**
SERVING SIZE **1 cup**
PREP TIME **10 mins**
COOK TIME **6 hrs 10 mins**
TOTAL TIME **6 hrs 20 mins**

  PROGRAM
Slow Cook

 PRESSURE
none

 RELEASE
none

½ cup 100% natural apple juice
½ cup barbecue sauce
2 tsp Sriracha sauce
1½ lbs (680g) boneless, skinless chicken thighs
1 small red onion, thinly sliced
1 green bell pepper, seeded and thinly sliced
¼ tsp kosher salt
¼ tsp freshly ground black pepper

1. Make the sauce by combining the apple juice, barbecue sauce, and Sriracha sauce in a small bowl. Mix well, and set aside.

2. Add the chicken thighs, onion, and bell pepper to the inner pot. Season with the salt and pepper.

3. Add the sauce to the pot. Using tongs, turn the chicken thighs and vegetables to thoroughly coat in the sauce.

4. Cover and lock the lid, but leave the steam release handle in the venting position. Select **Slow Cook (More)**, and then set the cook time for **6 hours**.

5. When the cook time is complete, remove the lid, select **Sauté**, and simmer until the sauce thickens (about 10 minutes). Use forks to shred the chicken, and then transfer to a serving platter. Serve hot.

Make it a meal by adding a 1 cup serving of brown rice (205 calories).

NUTRITION PER SERVING

Total fat **7g**	Cholesterol **148mg**	Carbohydrates **25g**	Sugars **20g**
Saturated fat **2g**	Sodium **448mg**	Dietary fiber **1g**	Protein **33g**

Lightened-Up Shrimp and Grits

Traditional shrimp and grits is loaded with fat, but this version cuts the fat and calories, and uses the flavor of sweet, earthy smoked paprika to replace fatty bacon.

PROGRAM
Sauté/Pressure Cook

PRESSURE
High

RELEASE
Natural/Quick

1 tbsp olive oil

2 tbsp unsalted butter, divided

12oz (340g) large raw shrimp, peeled and deveined

1 clove garlic, minced

½ cup chopped fire-roasted red peppers

½ tsp smoked paprika

½ tsp kosher salt

2 tsp chopped fresh thyme

½ tsp red pepper flakes

Juice of ½ lemon

½ cup coarse grits

2 cups water

½ cup grated sharp cheddar cheese

2 tbsp sliced scallions

1. Select **Sauté,** and add the olive oil and 1 tablespoon of the butter to the inner pot.

2. Add the shrimp and garlic to the pot, and sauté for 2 minutes. Add the roasted red pepper and season with the paprika, kosher salt, thyme, red pepper flakes, and lemon juice. Sauté for an additional 3–5 minutes, or until the shrimp is opaque, and then select **Cancel** to turn off the heat.

3. Transfer the shrimp and sauce to a large bowl. Cover with aluminum foil, and set aside.

4. Add the grits and the remaining butter to the pot, and then stir in the water.

5. Cover, lock the lid, and flip the steam release handle to the sealing position. Select **Pressure Cook (High)**, and set the cook time for **10 minutes**. When the cook time is complete, allow the pressure to release naturally for 10 minutes, and then quick release the remaining pressure.

6. Remove the lid, add the cheese, and stir until the cheese is melted and the grits are creamy.

7. Transfer to serving bowls and top each serving with the shrimp and sauce, and then garnish with the scallions. Serve hot.

NUTRITION PER SERVING

Total fat **13g**	Cholesterol **161mg**	Carbohydrates **19g**	Sugars **2g**
Saturated fat **6g**	Sodium **311mg**	Dietary fiber **2g**	Protein **21g**

Quick and Easy Vegetable Lasagna

Preparing lasagna can be time consuming, and often results in too much food. This lighter version yields a reasonable portion, and will become a weeknight staple.

PROGRAM
Sauté/Pressure Cook

PRESSURE
High

RELEASE
Natural

2 tsp olive oil

3 cups raw kale, washed and trimmed

1 cup sliced fresh mushrooms

Pinch of salt

½ tsp garlic powder

2 cups shredded part-skim mozzarella cheese

3 tbsp grated Parmesan cheese

1 cup part-skim ricotta cheese

1 large egg

½ tsp kosher salt

¼ tsp freshly ground black pepper

1¼ cups prepared marinara sauce, divided

6 no-boil lasagna noodles

3 tbsp chopped fresh basil

1. Spray a 1-quart (1l) soufflé dish with nonstick cooking spray. Use a clean paper towel to remove any excess spray from the dish.

2. Select **Sauté**, and add the olive oil to the inner pot. Add the kale and mushrooms, and sauté until the kale is slightly wilted and the mushrooms begin to soften (about 5 minutes). Season with the salt and garlic powder. Transfer to a bowl and set aside. Select **Cancel** to turn off the heat.

3. Carefully remove the inner pot from the base, wipe clean, and return to the base. Place the steam rack in the inner pot, and add 1 cup of water.

4. In a small bowl, combine the mozzarella and Parmesan. Mix well. In a separate medium bowl, combine the ricotta, egg, kosher salt, and pepper. Mix gently.

5. Add ¼ cup of the marinara sauce to the bottom of the prepared soufflé dish, and then add 2 noodles, half the vegetable mixture, ⅓ cup of the marinara, half the ricotta mixture, and a third of the mozzarella mixture. Repeat for the second layer, and then top with the two remaining noodles, remaining marinara, and remaining mozzarella mixture. Loosely cover the dish with aluminum foil, and lower into the pot.

6. Cover, lock the lid, and flip the steam release handle to the sealing position. Select **Pressure Cook (High)**, and set the cook time for **15 minutes**. When the cook time is complete, allow the pressure to release naturally (about 15 minutes).

7. Remove the lid, discard the foil, and allow the lasagna to cool slightly before garnishing with the fresh basil. Serve warm.

NUTRITION PER SERVING

Total fat **18g**	Cholesterol **98mg**	Carbohydrates **32g**	Sugars **11g**
Saturated fat **8g**	Sodium **632mg**	Dietary fiber **5g**	Protein **30g**

Turkey Bolognese with Penne

This robust ragu combines whole grains, fresh vegetables, and lean protein all in one pot. It's quickly become a family favorite in our house!

480 CALORIES PER SERVING

SERVES **6**
SERVING SIZE **2 cups**
PREP TIME **10 mins**
COOK TIME **15 mins**
TOTAL TIME **35 mins**

 PROGRAM **Sauté/Pressure Cook**

 PRESSURE **High**

RELEASE **Quick**

1. Select **Sauté**, and add the olive oil, carrot, celery, and garlic to the inner pot. Sauté for 2 minutes, or until the carrot and celery begin to soften, and the garlic becomes fragrant.

2. Add the kosher salt, fennel seed, and pepper to the pot, and then add the turkey breast. Sauté until the turkey breast is browned (about 5 minutes).

3. Pour the tomatoes over the turkey mixture, and then add the penne. Add the water, but do not stir the ingredients.

4. Cover, lock the lid, and flip the steam release handle to the sealing position. Select **Pressure Cook (High)**, and set the cook time for **8 minutes**. When the cook time is complete, quick release the pressure.

5. Remove the lid, stir well, and then transfer to a large serving platter. Sprinkle the Parmesan over top, and then garnish with the basil. Serve hot.

2 tsp olive oil
1 cup finely chopped carrot
1 cup finely chopped celery
2 cloves garlic, finely chopped
2 tsp kosher salt
1 tsp ground fennel seed
½ tsp freshly ground black pepper
1lb (450g) ground turkey breast
28oz (800g) can crushed tomatoes
1lb (450g) whole-grain penne pasta
3¼ cups water
½ cup grated Parmesan cheese
½ cup fresh basil leaves, roughly torn

Ground turkey breast is lower in fat and calories than regular ground turkey.

NUTRITION PER SERVING

Total fat **7g**	Cholesterol **55mg**	Carbohydrates **61g**	Sugars **8g**
Saturated fat **2g**	Sodium **601mg**	Dietary fiber **9g**	Protein **38g**

Chicken Sausage Paella

This lighter version of a classic Spanish recipe features chicken chorizo in place of pork chorizo. It's a simple, one-pot crowd-pleaser that only tastes exotic.

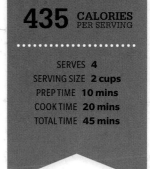
435 CALORIES PER SERVING

SERVES **4**
SERVING SIZE **2 cups**
PREP TIME **10 mins**
COOK TIME **20 mins**
TOTAL TIME **45 mins**

 PROGRAM
Sauté/Pressure Cook

 PRESSURE
High

RELEASE
Quick

1. Select **Sauté**, and add the olive oil to the inner pot. Add the chorizo and sauté for 3–5 minutes, or until the sausage browns and becomes crispy. Transfer to a plate, and set aside.

2. Add the rice, saffron, salsa, kosher salt, chicken stock, and water to the pot. Stir well.

3. Cover, lock the lid, and flip the steam release handle to the sealing position. Select **Pressure Cook (High)**, and set the cook time for **8 minutes**. When the cook time is complete, quick release the pressure.

4. Remove the lid, select **Sauté** and add the shrimp, olives, and peas to the pot. Cover, but do not lock the lid. Cook for an additional 5–7 minutes, stirring occasionally, until the shrimp becomes opaque.

5. Remove the lid, add the cooked sausage back to the inner pot, and stir well.

6. Transfer to serving bowls, and garnish with the lemon wedges. Serve hot.

1 tbsp olive oil

4oz (110g) chicken chorizo sausage, thinly sliced

1 cup Arborio rice

½ tsp saffron

½ cup salsa

½ tsp kosher salt

1 cup **From-Scratch Chicken Stock (see p100)** or low-sodium chicken stock

½ cup water

12oz (340g) uncooked shrimp, peeled and deveined

½ cup chopped green olives

1 cup frozen peas, thawed

Lemon wedges for serving

Make this vegetarian by substituting extra firm tofu for the sausage and shrimp.

NUTRITION PER SERVING

Total fat **12g**	Cholesterol **155mg**	Carbohydrates **52g**	Sugars **3g**
Saturated fat **3g**	Sodium **478mg**	Dietary fiber **3g**	Protein **33g**

Sweet and Spicy Pork Carnitas

Traditional versions of this dish are loaded with unhealthy fat and calories, but this flavorful, lighter version is infused with orange and smoked paprika.

 PROGRAM
Sauté/Pressure Cook

 PRESSURE
High

 RELEASE
Natural

½ cup orange juice

2 tbsp honey

½ tsp ground cumin

1 tsp smoked paprika

1½ tsp kosher salt, divided

2 x 1½lb (680g) pork tenderloins, each cut into three equal-sized pieces

½ medium red onion, sliced

1 bay leaf

1. In a small bowl, combine the orange juice, honey, cumin, paprika, and ½ teaspoon of the kosher salt, and stir continuously until the honey is completely dissolved. Season the pork shoulder with the remaining kosher salt.

2. Select **Sauté**, and add the tenderloin to the inner pot, followed by the onion. Sear for 2–3 minutes per side, or until the tenderloin is lightly browned on both sides. Add the orange juice mixture and bay leaf to the pot.

3. Cover, lock the lid, and flip the steam release handle to the sealing position. Select **Pressure Cook (High)**, and set the cook time for **30 minutes**. When the cook time is complete, allow the pressure to release naturally (about 15 minutes).

4. Remove the lid, and use forks to shred the pork. Select **Sauté**, and allow the carnitas to simmer until the sauce thickens slightly.

5. Select **Keep Warm** and serve the carnitas directly from the pot.

Serve with brown rice, on warm tortillas, or in salads or rice bowls.

NUTRITION PER SERVING

Total fat **4g**	Cholesterol **82mg**	Carbohydrates **7g**	Sugars **6g**
Saturated fat **1g**	Sodium **496mg**	Dietary fiber **0g**	Protein **35g**

Chicken Apricot Curry

This sweet and spicy chicken dish uses lite coconut milk, which contains less fat and calories than regular coconut milk. The Instant Pot makes this one quick and easy!

283 CALORIES PER SERVING

SERVES **4**
SERVING SIZE **1½ cups**
PREP TIME **5 mins**
COOK TIME **10 mins**
TOTAL TIME **25 mins**

PROGRAM
Sauté/Pressure Cook

PRESSURE
High

RELEASE
Quick

1. Select **Sauté**, and add the olive oil to the inner pot.

2. Add the onion, garlic, curry powder, and red pepper flakes to the pot. Sauté for 3 minutes. Add the chicken strips and toss to coat.

3. Add the soy sauce and apricots, followed by the coconut milk, tomato sauce, and honey. Stir well.

4. Cover, lock the lid, and flip the steam release handle to the sealing position. Select **Pressure Cook (High)**, and set the cook time for **4 minutes**.

5. While the chicken is cooking, combine the cornstarch and water in a small bowl, and stir until a smooth consistency is achieved.

6. When the cook time is complete, quick release the pressure and remove the lid. Select **Sauté**, and bring the ingredients to a simmer. Stir in the cornstarch mixture and continue to cook until the sauce is thickened (about 3 minutes).

7. Transfer to serving bowls and garnish with the cilantro, cashews, and a squeeze of fresh lime juice. Serve hot.

2 tsp olive oil
½ cup chopped yellow onion
1 clove garlic, finely chopped
2 tsp curry powder
¼ tsp red pepper flakes
1 lb (450g) boneless, skinless chicken breasts, cut into 2-inch (5cm) strips
2 tsp reduced-sodium soy sauce
6 dried apricots, roughly chopped
½ cup lite coconut milk
½ cup tomato sauce
1 tbsp honey
2 tsp cornstarch
1 tbsp water
¼ cup chopped fresh cilantro
¼ cup chopped cashews
Lime wedges for serving

This is delicious served with warmed flatbread or steamed brown rice.

NUTRITION PER SERVING

Total fat **12g**	Cholesterol **73mg**	Carbohydrates **20g**	Sugars **14g**
Saturated fat **3g**	Sodium **283mg**	Dietary fiber **2g**	Protein **26g**

Jalepeño-Cheese Tamales

This labor of love is well worth the effort, and the cook time is slashed thanks to the Instant Pot. These are delicious, so good for you, and the ingredients are simple!

 PROGRAM
Pressure Cook

 PRESSURE
High

RELEASE
Natural

1 package corn husks
3 cups masa harina flour
1 tsp kosher salt
1 tsp baking powder
½ tsp dried thyme leaves
1 tsp chipotle chili powder
1 cup shredded cotija cheese
½ cup pickled jalapeños
2½ cups water
½ cup olive oil
Verde sauce, for serving

1. Soften the corn husks by filling a large bowl with hot water, adding the husks to the bowl, and soaking for a minimum of 30 minutes. While the husks are soaking, combine the masa flour, kosher salt, baking powder, thyme, and chili powder in a large bowl. Mix well. In a separate medium bowl, combine the cotija cheese and jalapeños. Mix well.

2. Add the water to the bowl containing the dough ingredients. Using a hand or stand mixer, mix the dough on low speed until the ingredients are well combined. Add the olive oil, increase the mixer speed to medium, and continue to mix until a soft dough forms. (If the dough is too dry, add more water, one tablespoon at a time, until the desired consistency is achieved.)

3. Assemble the tamales by laying a corn husk on a flat surface, with the smaller end closest to you. Tear a thin strip from the long edge of the husk and set aside (this will be used to tie the tamale closed). Place 2 tablespoons of the masa dough in the center of the husk, and then top with a heaping spoonful of the jalapeño and cheese mixture. Fold the long sides of the corn husk inward so they overlap, and then fold the narrow end upward to form a pouch. Secure the tamale with the reserved strip of husk. Repeat with the remaining ingredients.

4. Place the steam rack in the inner pot and add 1½ cups of water. Arrange the tamales upright on the steam rack. Cover, lock the lid, and flip the steam release handle to the sealing position. Select **Pressure Cook (High)**, and set the cook time for **40 minutes**. When the cook time is complete, allow the pressure to release naturally (about 20 minutes). Transfer to a serving platter, and repeat the cooking process with the remaining tamales. Top with a spoonful of verde sauce. Serve warm.

Find masa flour, corn husks, and cotija cheese in the international sections of grocery stores.

NUTRITION PER SERVING

Total fat **5g**	Cholesterol **3mg**	Carbohydrates **8g**	Sugars **0g**
Saturated fat **1g**	Sodium **129mg**	Dietary fiber **1g**	Protein **2g**

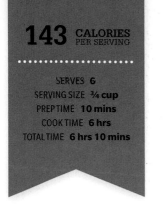

143 CALORIES PER SERVING

SERVES **6**
SERVING SIZE **¾ cup**
PREP TIME **10 mins**
COOK TIME **6 hrs**
TOTAL TIME **6 hrs 10 mins**

Slow Cooker Chicken Cacciatore

This simple and delicious dish is high in protein, low in fat, and rich in antioxidants. Who doesn't love an easy, healthy dinner where the slow cooker does all the work?

PROGRAM
Slow Cook

PRESSURE
none

RELEASE
none

1½ lbs (680g) boneless, skinless chicken thighs

½ medium red onion, thinly sliced

2 green bell peppers, thinly sliced and seeds removed

½ cup prepared marinara sauce

¼ cup **From-Scratch Chicken Stock (see p100)** or low-sodium chicken stock

1 clove garlic, thinly sliced

¾ tsp kosher salt

Pinch red pepper flakes

¼ cup chopped fresh basil

1. Combine the chicken thighs, onion, bell peppers, marinara sauce, chicken stock, garlic, kosher salt, and red pepper flakes in the inner pot. Toss gently.

2. Cover and lock the lid, but leave the steam release handle in the venting position. Select **Slow Cook (More)**, and set the cook time for **6 hours**.

3. When the cook time is complete, remove the lid and use forks to shred the chicken. Transfer to a serving bowl and garnish with the basil. Serve warm.

Serve with pasta, polenta, potatoes, or a crusty whole grain bread.

NUTRITION PER SERVING

Total fat **4g**	Cholesterol **99mg**	Carbohydrates **8g**	Sugars **2g**
Saturated fat **1g**	Sodium **325mg**	Dietary fiber **2g**	Protein **23g**

Braised Short Ribs

Cooking this famously tough cut in the Instant Pot forces it into tender, savory submission. Beef contains vital minerals, and helps promote a healthy immune system.

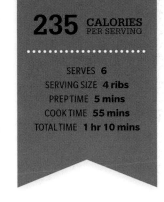

235 CALORIES PER SERVING

SERVES **6**
SERVING SIZE **4 ribs**
PREP TIME **5 mins**
COOK TIME **55 mins**
TOTAL TIME **1 hr 10 mins**

 PROGRAM
Sauté/Pressure Cook

 PRESSURE
High

RELEASE
Natural/Quick

1. Make the sauce by combining the ketchup, molasses, soy sauce, and brown sugar in a small bowl. Mix well, and set aside. Season the short ribs with the kosher salt and pepper.

2. Select **Sauté**, add the short ribs to the inner pot, and sauté for 3–5 minutes, or until the ribs are browned on both sides.

3. Add the sauce to the pot. Using tongs, thoroughly coat the ribs in the sauce.

4. Cover, lock the lid, and flip the steam release handle to the sealing position. Select **Pressure Cook (High)**, and set the cook time for **40 minutes**. When the cook time is complete, allow the pressure to release naturally for 10 minutes, and then quick release the remaining pressure.

5. Using a slotted spoon, transfer the ribs to a serving platter. Serve warm.

2 tbsp ketchup

1 tbsp molasses

2 tsp reduced-sodium soy sauce

2 tsp light brown sugar

2lbs (1kg) boneless beef short ribs

½ tsp kosher salt

½ tsp freshly ground black pepper

NUTRITION PER SERVING

Total fat **10g**	Cholesterol **106mg**	Carbohydrates **6g**	Sugars **5g**
Saturated fat **4g**	Sodium **326mg**	Dietary fiber **0g**	Protein **30g**

336 CALORIES
PER SERVING

SERVES **10**
SERVING SIZE **3oz (85g)**
beef + 2 cups vegetables
PREP TIME **15 mins**
COOK TIME **1 hr 45 mins**
TOTAL TIME **2 hrs 25 mins**

Corned Beef and Cabbage

Offering plenty of protein, B-vitamins, and minerals, this classic recipe is healthier than you might think, and it can be made in half the time in the Instant Pot!

PROGRAM **Pressure Cook**	PRESSURE **High**

RELEASE
Natural/Quick

3lbs (1.4kg) corned beef brisket, rinsed, trimmed, and patted dry

1 tsp mustard seed

1 tsp dill seed

1 tsp granulated garlic

1 cup water

1 head green cabbage, cored and cut into 6 wedges

4 large carrots, peeled and cut into large chunks

9 small red potatoes (about 12oz), quartered

1. Place the brisket in the inner pot, and add the mustard seed, dill seed, granulated garlic, and water.

2. Cover, lock the lid, and switch the steam release handle to the sealing position. Select **Pressure Cook (High)**, and set the cook time for **1 hour 10 minutes**. When the cook time is compete, allow the pressure to release naturally (about 30 minutes).

3. Remove the lid, transfer the brisket to a large plate, and cover with aluminum foil. Remove and discard all but 1 cup of the cooking liquid from the inner pot, and then add the cabbage, carrots, and potatoes.

4. Cover, lock the lid, and switch the steam release handle to the sealing position. Select **Pressure Cook (High)**, and set the cook time for **3 minutes**. When the cook time is complete, quick release the pressure.

5. Using a slotted spoon, transfer the vegetables to a serving platter. Transfer the corned beef to a cutting board and cut into thin slices, and then transfer to the serving platter. Serve warm.

NUTRITION PER SERVING

Total fat **21g**	Cholesterol **73mg**	Carbohydrates **16g**	Sugars **6g**
Saturated fat **6g**	Sodium **890mg**	Dietary fiber **5g**	Protein **22g**

Coffee-Rubbed Brisket

Brisket is famously tough, but the Instant Pot makes it fork-tender. The highlights of this recipe are an aromatic spice rub, and a rendered jus that's perfect for dipping.

228 CALORIES PER SERVING

SERVES **6**
SERVING SIZE **4oz (110g)**
PREP TIME **2 hrs 10 mins**
COOK TIME **1 hr 19 mins**
TOTAL TIME **3 hrs 45 mins**

PROGRAM
Sauté/Pressure Cook

PRESSURE
High

RELEASE
Natural

1. Make the sauce by combining the water, ketchup, soy sauce, and brown sugar in a medium bowl. Mix well, and set aside.

2. Make the spice rub by combining the coffee, kosher salt, pepper, and rosemary in a medium bowl. Mix well.

3. Using clean hands, apply the spice rub to the brisket, and then place it in a resealable freezer bag. Seal the bag, and squeeze to massage the rub into the brisket. Place in the refrigerator for a minimum of 2 hours to allow the brisket to absorb the flavors of the rub, or for up to 24 hours to develop a deeper flavor.

4. Remove the brisket from the refrigerator and discard the bag. Slice the brisket in half, slicing against the grain.

5. Select **Sauté**, place the two halves in the pot, fat-sides-down, and sear for 2 minutes per side. Add the sauce to the pot.

6. Cover, lock the lid, and flip the steam release handle to the sealing position. Select **Pressure Cook (High)**, and set the cook time for **1 hour**. When the cook time is complete, allow the pressure to release naturally (about 15 minutes).

7. Remove the lid, and carefully transfer the brisket to a cutting board. Cut away the layer of fat from the bottom of each piece, and then slice the halves against the grain and into 2-inch (5cm) slices.

8. Transfer to a serving platter. Serve warm, with the jus served on the side for dipping.

½ cup water
2 tbsp ketchup
2 tbsp reduced-sodium soy sauce
1 tbsp lightly packed, light brown sugar
2 tbsp finely ground coffee
1 tsp kosher salt
½ tsp freshly ground black pepper
1 tsp dried rosemary
2½ lbs (1.13kg) beef brisket

NUTRITION PER SERVING

| Total fat **10g** | Cholesterol **94mg** | Carbohydrates **4g** | Sugars **3g** |
| Saturated fat **3g** | Sodium **251mg** | Dietary fiber **0g** | Protein **31g** |

Chinese Five-Spice Sticky Ribs

Fall-apart ribs are less than an hour away! Cooking these sweet and spicy ribs under pressure helps render much of the fat away from the meat, and cut the calories.

387 CALORIES PER SERVING

SERVES **6**
SERVING SIZE **3 ribs**
PREP TIME **10 mins**
COOK TIME **32 mins**
TOTAL TIME **1 hr**

PROGRAM
Pressure Cook

PRESSURE
High

RELEASE
Quick

1. Make the five-spice powder by combining the cinnamon stick, cloves, fennel seeds, star anise, and Szechuan peppercorns in a spice grinder. Grind until a fine powder is formed.

2. Place the ribs in a large bowl. Using clean hands, liberally apply the five-spice powder to the ribs, and then season with the kosher salt. Add the garlic and ¼ cup of the hoisin sauce to the bowl. Toss the ribs in the sauce to coat.

3. Arrange the ribs upright in the inner pot. Add the pomegranate juice to the bottom of the pot.

4. Cover, lock the lid, and flip the steam release handle to the sealing position. Select **Pressure Cook (High)**, and set the cook time for **28 minutes**.

5. While the ribs are cooking, preheat the broiler to high and line a large sheet pan with aluminum foil.

6. When the cook time for the ribs is complete, quick release the pressure, remove the lid, and carefully transfer the ribs to the sheet pan. Brush with the remaining hoisin sauce.

7. Place on the top rack in the broiler for 3–4 minutes, watching the ribs carefully to ensure they don't burn. Allow to cool for 10 minutes before transferring to a cutting board and cutting into individual ribs. Serve warm.

1 tbsp Chinese 5-spice powder
4lb (1.8kg) rack pork spare ribs, cut into four equal-sized pieces
1 tsp kosher salt
2 cloves garlic, finely chopped
½ cup hoisin sauce, divided
¼ cup pomegranate juice

For the Chinese five-spice powder:
1 cinnamon stick
1 tsp whole cloves
1 tbsp fennel seeds
4 whole star anise
1 tbsp Szechuan peppercorns

NUTRITION PER SERVING

Total fat **13g**	Cholesterol **168mg**	Carbohydrates **18g**	Sugars **13g**
Saturated fat **5g**	Sodium **533mg**	Dietary fiber **0g**	Protein **47g**

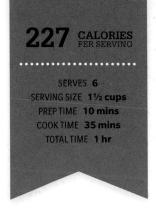

227 CALORIES PER SERVING

SERVES **6**
SERVING SIZE **1½ cups**
PREP TIME **10 mins**
COOK TIME **35 mins**
TOTAL TIME **1 hr**

Vegetarian Shepherd's Pie

Traditional shepherd's pie is loaded with fatty meat and buttery mashed potatoes, but this delicious meat-free version contains a fraction of the fat and calories.

PROGRAM
Pressure Cook/Sauté

PRESSURE
High

RELEASE
Quick

2lbs (1kg) sweet potatoes, peeled, and diced into 1-inch (2.5cm) pieces

1 tsp kosher salt, divided

½ cup nonfat Greek yogurt

2 tbsp olive oil, divided

10oz (285g) cremini mushrooms, stems removed and quartered

1 cup chopped carrots

1 cup chopped celery

1 cup chopped yellow onion

2 cloves garlic, minced

2 tsp dried thyme leaves

½ tsp freshly ground black pepper

½ cup **Vegetable Broth (see p101)** or low-sodium vegetable broth

1 tbsp all-purpose flour

2 tbsp water

½ cup frozen peas

1. Preheat the oven to 375°F (191°C), and line a large baking sheet with parchment paper. Place the steam rack in the inner pot and add 1 cup water. Add the sweet potatoes, and season with ¼ teaspoon kosher salt.

2. Cover, lock the lid, and flip the steam release handle to the sealing position. Select **Pressure Cook (High)**, and set the cook time for **9 minutes**. When the cook time is complete, quick release the pressure, remove the lid, and carefully transfer the potatoes to a large bowl. Add the Greek yogurt, and use a potato masher to mash the ingredients until a smooth consistency is achieved. Set aside.

3. Wipe the inner pot clean with a paper towel. Select **Sauté**, and add 1 tablespoon of the olive oil, followed by the mushrooms, carrots, celery, onion, garlic, thyme, pepper, and remaining kosher salt. Sauté for 3 minutes, and then stir in the vegetable broth.

4. Cover, lock the lid, and flip the steam release handle to the sealing position. Select **Pressure Cook (High)**, and set the cook time for **1 minute**. When the cook time is complete, quick release the pressure, remove the lid, and once again select **Sauté** to bring the ingredients to a simmer. Meanwhile, combine the flour, water, and remaining 1 tablespoon olive oil in a small bowl. Whisk ingredients to form a paste. Add the flour mixture to the pot and stir continuously until the sauce thickens, about 2 minutes, and then stir in the frozen peas. Select **Cancel** to turn off the heat.

5. Transfer the vegetable mixture to a 9-inch (23cm) pie plate, and spoon the sweet potatoes over top of the vegetables. Transfer the plate to the baking sheet and bake for 20 minutes. Serve warm.

NUTRITION PER SERVING

Total fat **5g**	Cholesterol **0mg**	Carbohydrates **41g**	Sugars **11g**
Saturated fat **1g**	Sodium **468mg**	Dietary fiber **11g**	Protein **7g**

Light and Lean Taco Bowl

This quick and healthy meal features freshly squeezed lime juice and Greek yogurt to create a light, refreshing meal that's satisfying, but doesn't include a ton of calories.

390 CALORIES PER SERVING

SERVES **4**
SERVING SIZE **1 bowl**
PREP TIME **5 mins**
COOK TIME **11 mins**
TOTAL TIME **22 mins**

 PROGRAM
Sauté/Pressure Cook

 PRESSURE
High

 RELEASE
Quick

1. Select **Sauté**, and add the ground beef, onion, and bell pepper to the inner pot. Sauté for 2–3 minutes, or until the beef begins to brown.

2. Add the kosher salt, cumin, chili powder, and celery salt to the pot. Stir well, and sauté for an additional 3 minutes.

3. Cover, lock the lid, and flip the steam release handle to the sealing position. Select **Pressure Cook (High)**, and set the cook time for **5 minutes**. When the cook time is complete, quick release the pressure.

4. Remove the lid and add the black beans. Stir well to combine.

5. To serve, add 2 cups of the greens, ¼ cup of the carrots, and ¼ cup of the diced avocado to a serving bowl, and top with 1 cup of the taco filling, ⅛ cup of the Greek yogurt, and ¼ cup of the pico de gallo. Repeat with the remaining servings. Serve warm, with a lime wedge on the side.

1 pound 90%-lean ground beef
½ cup chopped onion
1 medium bell pepper (red or orange), seeded and chopped
½ tsp kosher salt
1 tsp ground cumin
½ tsp chili powder
¼ tsp celery salt
1 cup canned black beans, rinsed and drained
8 cups mixed salad greens
1 cup grated carrots
1 avocado, diced
½ cup **Homemade Greek Yogurt (see p33)** or low-fat Greek yogurt
1 cup pico de gallo
Lime wedges for serving

NUTRITION PER SERVING

Total fat **18g**	Cholesterol **76mg**	Carbohydrates **29g**	Sugars **11g**
Saturated fat **6g**	Sodium **383mg**	Dietary fiber **9g**	Protein **31g**

327 CALORIES PER SERVING

SERVES **6**
SERVING SIZE **1⅓ cups**
PREP TIME **10 mins**
COOK TIME **4 mins**
TOTAL TIME **35 mins**

Gluten-Free Creamy Pesto Pasta

This quick and healthy, gluten-free pasta dish can be tossed together at the last minute for unexpected guests, or for a kid-friendly weeknight dinner.

PROGRAM
Pressure Cook

PRESSURE
High

RELEASE
Quick

1lb (450g) gluten-free, brown rice linguine
¼ tsp kosher salt
4 cups water
¼ cup grated Parmesan cheese

For the pesto sauce:
2 cups fresh arugula
2 cups fresh basil leaves
Juice of ½ lemon
2 tbsp chopped walnuts
⅓ cup olive oil
Salt and freshly ground black pepper

1. To make the pesto sauce, combine the arugula, basil, lemon juice, and walnuts in a food processor. Begin pulsing the ingredients, while continuously adding the olive oil. Continue pulsing until a smooth, uniform consistency is achieved.

2. Combine the linguine, kosher salt, and water in the inner pot. Stir well.

3. Cover, lock the lid, and flip the steam release handle to the sealing position. Select **Pressure Cook (High)**, and set the cook time for **4 minutes**. When the cook time is complete, quick release the pressure. (If the cooked pasta is too sticky, remove from the pot, rinse, drain thoroughly, and return to the pot.)

4. Open the lid, and add the Parmesan and 2 tablespoons of the pesto sauce. Mix well.

5. Allow to cool and thicken in the pot for 10 minutes before transferring to a serving platter. Season with salt and pepper. Serve warm.

Store leftover pesto in the fridge for up to 3 days, or freeze up to 3 months.

NUTRITION PER SERVING

Total fat **7g**	Cholesterol **4mg**	Carbohydrates **60g**	Sugars **4g**
Saturated fat **2g**	Sodium **83mg**	Dietary fiber **4g**	Protein **7g**

424 CALORIES
PER SERVING

SERVES **6**
SERVING SIZE
1 cup + 1 meatball
PREP TIME **15 mins**
COOK TIME **10 mins**
TOTAL TIME **50 mins**

Spaghetti and Meatballs

You'll have this simple and hearty Italian dinner on the table in less than an hour. Cooking the tomatoes under pressure helps boost the antioxidant content.

 PROGRAM
Sauté/Pressure Cook

 PRESSURE
High

RELEASE
Quick

1lb (450g) 90% lean ground beef

1 large egg, beaten

4 tbsp Italian-seasoned breadcrumbs

1¼ tsp kosher salt, divided

½ tsp freshly ground black pepper, divided

1 tbsp olive oil

1 clove garlic, minced

½ small yellow onion, finely chopped

½ tsp ground fennel seed

28oz (800g) can crushed tomatoes, divided

10oz (285g) spaghetti, broken in half

1 cup water

4 tbsp grated Parmesan cheese

1. In a medium bowl, combine the ground beef, egg, breadcrumbs, 1 teaspoon of the kosher salt, and ¼ teaspoon of the pepper. Using clean hands, mix the ingredients well and form into 6 equal-sized meatballs.

2. Select **Sauté**, and add the olive oil to the inner pot. Add the garlic and onion, season with the remaining salt and pepper, and then add the fennel seed. Sauté for 2 minutes, and then stir in 2½ cups of the crushed tomatoes and cook for an additional 3 minutes, stirring frequently. Press **Cancel** to turn off the heat.

3. Carefully add the meatballs to the bottom of the pot in an even layer. Next add the pasta in an even layer over the meatballs, followed by the remaining crushed tomatoes, and then the water.

4. Cover, lock the lid, and flip the steam release handle to the sealing position. Select **Pressure Cook (High)**, and set the cook time for **5 minutes**. When the cook time is complete, quick release the pressure.

5. Remove the lid, transfer to a large serving platter, and allow to cool for 10 minutes before sprinkling the Parmesan over top. Serve warm.

Make this gluten-free by substituting gluten-free breadcrumbs, and brown rice spaghetti.

NUTRITION PER SERVING

Total fat **13g**	Cholesterol **84mg**	Carbohydrates **50g**	Sugars **8g**
Saturated fat **5g**	Sodium **598mg**	Dietary fiber **4g**	Protein **27g**

Open-Faced Sloppy Joes

This deliciously messy classic isn't just for kids!
This version reduces the sodium to half of what
is typically found in store-bought sloppy joe sauces.

261 CALORIES PER SERVING

SERVES **6**
SERVING SIZE **1**
PREP TIME **5 mins**
COOK TIME **11 mins**
TOTAL TIME **25 mins**

PROGRAM
Sauté/Pressure Cook

PRESSURE
High

RELEASE
Quick

1. Select **Sauté**, and add the ground beef to the inner pot. Sauté for
   2–3 minutes, or until the beef is lightly browned.

2. Add the kosher salt, pepper, cumin, ketchup, brown sugar, and soy
   sauce to the pot. Sauté for an additional 3 minutes, and then stir in
   the diced tomato.

3. Cover, lock the lid, and flip the steam release handle to the sealing
   position. Select **Pressure Cook (High)**, and set the cook time for
   5 minutes. When the cook time is complete, quick release the
   pressure, remove the lid, and stir well.

4. Arrange the rolls, open sides up, on a large serving platter. Top each
   roll with ⅓ cup of the baby spinach and ¾ cup of the sloppy joe filling,
   and then sprinkle 1 tablespoon of Monterey Jack over top of each roll.
   Serve warm.

1lb (450g) 90% lean
  ground beef
¼ tsp kosher salt
¼ tsp freshly ground
  black pepper
1 tsp ground cumin
¼ cup ketchup
¼ cup light brown sugar
1 tsp reduced-sodium
  soy sauce
1 plum tomato, diced
3 whole-grain rolls,
  split into halves
2 cups fresh baby spinach
½ cup shredded
  Monterey Jack cheese

NUTRITION PER SERVING

Total fat **10g**	Cholesterol **54mg**	Carbohydrates **24g**	Sugars **13g**
Saturated fat **4g**	Sodium **306mg**	Dietary fiber **2g**	Protein **19g**

Lighter-Than-Takeout Chicken with Broccoli

In the time it takes to dig out the menu you can make this lighter version of a takeout favorite. This version cuts the fat and sodium, and uses brown rice instead of white.

 PROGRAM
Sauté/Pressure Cook

 PRESSURE
High

 RELEASE
Quick

1. In a small bowl, make the sauce by combining the sesame oil, chicken stock, soy sauce, rice vinegar, and honey. Whisk to combine, and then set aside.

2. Select **Sauté**, and add the canola oil to the inner pot. Add the chicken strips and sauté for 3–5 minutes, or until the chicken is browned. Add the sauce and stir until the chicken is thoroughly coated in the sauce.

3. Cover, lock the lid, and flip the steam release handle to the sealing position. Select **Pressure Cook (High)**, and set the cook time for **4 minutes**.

4. While the chicken is cooking, combine the cornstarch and water in a small bowl. Mix well.

5. When the cook time for the chicken is complete, quick release the pressure, remove the lid, and once again select **Sauté**. Bring the ingredients to a simmer, and then stir in the cornstarch mixture and add the broccoli. Cook for an additional 3 minutes, or until the sauce thickens and the broccoli is slightly tender.

6. Add 1 cup of the cooked brown rice to a serving bowl and top with 2 cups of the chicken and broccoli. Garnish with the green onion and cashews. Serve hot.

1 tsp sesame oil

¼ cup **From-Scratch Chicken Stock (see p100)** or low-sodium chicken stock

¼ cup low-sodium soy sauce

2 tbsp rice vinegar

1 tbsp honey

1 tbsp canola oil

1lb (450g) boneless, skinless chicken breasts, cut into 2-inch (5cm) strips

1 tbsp cornstarch

2 tbsp water

4 cups fresh broccoli florets

4 cups cooked brown rice, for serving

2 tbsp chopped green onion

3 tbsp chopped cashews

Make this gluten-free by using tamari instead of soy sauce.

NUTRITION PER SERVING

Total fat **13g**	Cholesterol **73mg**	Carbohydrates **63g**	Sugars **9g**
Saturated fat **2g**	Sodium **472mg**	Dietary fiber **6g**	Protein **33g**

178 CALORIES PER SERVING

SERVES **4**
SERVING SIZE **1 cup**
PREP TIME **5 mins**
COOK TIME **8 mins**
TOTAL TIME **25 mins**

Chicken Sausage with Peppers and Onions

This healthier take on sausage with peppers and onions is one of my favorite go-to dinners. Serve with brown rice or whole grain pasta for a quick and satisfying meal.

 PROGRAM
Sauté/Pressure Cook

 PRESSURE
High

RELEASE
Quick

2 tsp olive oil

12 oz (340g) fully cooked, Italian-style chicken sausage, sliced into ¼-inch (.5cm) pieces

2 green bell peppers, seeded and sliced

1 large red onion, sliced

½ cup canned diced tomatoes

¼ tsp kosher salt

2 tsp chopped fresh thyme

2 tbsp chopped fresh parsley

1. Select **Sauté**, and add the olive oil to the inner pot. Add the sausage and sauté for 2–3 minutes, or until the sausage begins to brown.

2. Add the peppers, onion, tomatoes, kosher salt, and thyme. Stir well.

3. Cover, lock the lid, and flip the steam release handle to the sealing position. Select **Pressure Cook (High)**, and set the cook time for **5 minutes**. When the cook time is complete, quick release the pressure.

4. Open the lid, stir, and allow to cool slightly before transferring to a serving bowl and topping with the chopped parsley. Serve warm.

Use the leftovers for topping a pizza, or for filling quesadillas.

NUTRITION PER SERVING

Total fat **9g**	Cholesterol **69mg**	Carbohydrates **10g**	Sugars **4g**
Saturated fat **3g**	Sodium **554mg**	Dietary fiber **2g**	Protein **15g**

Best-Ever Vegetarian Tacos

These lighter tacos are a refreshing change from meat and cheese tacos, and feature vitamin-packed, fiber-rich vegetables served in whole-grain corn tortillas.

274 CALORIES PER SERVING

SERVES **6**
SERVING SIZE **2**
PREP TIME **10 mins**
COOK TIME **5 mins**
TOTAL TIME **20 mins**

PROGRAM
Sauté/Pressure Cook

PRESSURE
High

RELEASE
Quick

1. Make the verde sauce by combining the avocado, lime juice, cilantro, jalapeño, vinegar, honey, 1 teaspoon of the kosher salt, onion, and water in a blender. Blend for 30 seconds, or until a smooth consistency is achieved. Set aside.

2. Select **Sauté**, and add the olive oil, garlic, and cumin seed to the inner pot. Add the cauliflower, season with the remaining kosher salt and cayenne pepper, and toss to coat. Add the vegetable broth.

3. Cover, lock the lid, and flip the steam release handle to the sealing position. Select **Pressure Cook (High)**, and set the cook time for **1 minute**. When the cook time is complete, quick release the pressure.

4. Remove the lid and add the black beans. Stir well.

5. Warm the tortillas and arrange on a serving platter. Add equal amounts of the taco filling to each tortilla, and then top each with a spoonful of the green sauce. Serve warm.

1 tbsp olive oil
1 clove garlic, finely chopped
2 tsp cumin seed
1 large head cauliflower, trimmed and chopped
Pinch cayenne pepper
½ cup **Vegetable Broth (see p101)** or low-sodium vegetable broth
2 cups canned black beans, rinsed and drained
12 x 6-inch (15.25cm) whole-grain corn tortillas
Green sauce, for serving

For the verde sauce:
1 avocado
Juice of 1 lime
2 cups fresh cilantro
1 jalapeño pepper, stem removed
2 tbsp white vinegar
1 tbsp honey
1½ tsp kosher salt, divided
¼ white onion
1 cup water

NUTRITION PER SERVING

Total fat **6g**	Cholesterol **0mg**	Carbohydrates **49g**	Sugars **8g**
Saturated fat **1g**	Sodium **346mg**	Dietary fiber **12g**	Protein **11g**

Soups & Stews

Curry Shrimp Chowder

One serving of this rich, satisfying soup has less than 300 calories. It's a symphony of exotic flavors, with the secret ingredient being high-protein almond butter.

PROGRAM **Sauté/Pressure Cook**	PRESSURE **High**

RELEASE **Quick**

1 tbsp olive oil

1 medium red onion, chopped

1 medium green bell pepper, seeded and chopped

½ cup chopped celery

2 garlic cloves, minced

2 tsp minced ginger

½ tsp kosher salt

1 tbsp curry powder

1 cup canned tomato sauce

3 cups **From-Scratch Chicken Stock (see p100)** or low-sodium chicken stock

3 tbsp almond butter

12oz (340g) large uncooked shrimp, peeled, deveined, and tails removed

1 cup frozen shelled edamame, thawed

3 cups baby spinach leaves

½ cup chopped scallions

1. Select **Sauté**, and add the olive oil to the inner pot. Add the onion, bell pepper, and celery, and sauté for 2–3 minutes, or until the ingredients begin to soften.

2. Add the garlic, ginger, kosher salt, and curry powder, and sauté for an additional 3 minutes. Add the tomato sauce, chicken stock, and almond butter. Whisk until the ingredients are well combined.

3. Cover, lock the lid, and flip the steam release handle to the sealing position. Select **Pressure Cook (High)**, and set the cook time for **5 minutes**. When the cook time is complete, quick release the pressure.

4. Remove the lid, and add the shrimp and edamame. Mix well. Select **Sauté** and cook for 5–7 minutes, or until the shrimp are opaque, and then stir in the spinach.

5. Ladle the chowder into serving bowls and top with the chopped scallions. Serve hot.

NUTRITION PER SERVING

Total fat **13g**	Cholesterol **107mg**	Carbohydrates **17g**	Sugars **5g**
Saturated fat **1g**	Sodium **654mg**	Dietary fiber **6g**	Protein **24g**

Skinny Cheeseburger Soup

Cheeseburger soup? One taste of this recipe and you'll be a believer! With 15 grams of protein and only 208 calories per serving, this soup will satisfy any big burger craving.

208 CALORIES PER SERVING

SERVES **6**
SERVING SIZE **1 cup**
PREP TIME **10 mins**
COOK TIME **22 mins**
TOTAL TIME **40 mins**

PROGRAM
Sauté/Pressure Cook

PRESSURE
High

RELEASE
Natural/Quick

1. Select **Sauté**, and add the ground beef to the inner pot. Brown for 5 minutes, stirring frequently, and then add the onion, carrot, kosher salt, and pepper. Sauté for an additional 2 minutes.

2. Sprinkle the flour into the pot, and toss the ingredients well to coat. Add the potato and chicken stock, and stir well to combine.

3. Cover, lock the lid, and flip the steam release handle to the sealing position. Select **Pressure Cook (High)**, and set the cook time for **5 minutes**. When the cook time is complete, allow the pressure to release naturally for 10 minutes, and then quick release the remaining pressure.

4. Remove the lid, stir in the milk and cheese, and continue stirring until the cheese is melted and a smooth, creamy consistency is achieved. Ladle the soup into serving bowls and top with the lettuce. Serve immediately.

8oz (225g) 90% lean ground beef

½ medium yellow onion, chopped

1 cup roughly chopped carrot

½ tsp kosher salt

¼ tsp freshly ground black pepper

2 tbsp all-purpose flour

1 medium russet potato, peeled and diced

2 cups **From-Scratch Chicken Stock (see p100)** or low-sodium chicken stock

½ cup whole milk

1 cup shredded cheddar cheese

2 cups shredded iceberg lettuce, for serving

NUTRITION PER SERVING

Total fat **11g**	Cholesterol **47mg**	Carbohydrates **14g**	Sugars **3g**
Saturated fat **5g**	Sodium **298mg**	Dietary fiber **2g**	Protein **15g**

208 CALORIES
PER SERVING

SERVES **4**
SERVING SIZE **1½ cups**
PREP TIME **10 mins**
COOK TIME **35 mins**
TOTAL TIME **1 hr**

Sweet Potato Chili

Sweet potato, black beans, and hearty vegetables give this vegetarian chili flavor, texture, and a gorgeous color, as well as 8 grams of hunger-fighting fiber per serving.

 PROGRAM
Sauté/Pressure Cook

 PRESSURE
High

RELEASE
Natural

2 tsp canola oil

1 cup chopped yellow onion

1 clove garlic, finely chopped

1½ tsp chili powder

½ tsp ground cumin

28oz (800g) can
diced tomatoes

15oz (420g) can black beans,
rinsed and drained

1 medium green bell
pepper, seeded and diced

1 medium sweet potato,
peeled and diced

1 tsp kosher salt

¾ cup frozen corn kernels

1. Select **Sauté**, and add the canola oil to the inner pot. Add the onion and garlic. Sauté for 2 minutes, or until the garlic is fragrant, and the onion is soft and translucent.

2. Add the chili powder and cumin, followed by the tomatoes, black beans, bell pepper, sweet potato, and kosher salt. Stir well.

3. Cover, lock the lid, and flip the steam release handle to the sealing position. Select **Pressure Cook (High)**, and set the cook time for **15 minutes**. When the cook time is complete, allow the pressure to release naturally (about 20 minutes).

4. Remove the lid and stir in the corn. Ladle the chili into serving bowls. Serve hot.

Works perfect for a meatless Monday dinner, or even a gameday spread.

NUTRITION PER SERVING

Total fat **4g**	Cholesterol **0mg**	Carbohydrates **38g**	Sugars **12g**
Saturated fat **0g**	Sodium **566mg**	Dietary fiber **8g**	Protein **9g**

127 CALORIES PER SERVING

SERVES **4**
SERVING SIZE **1 cup**
PREP TIME **5 mins**
COOK TIME **18 mins**
TOTAL TIME **35 mins**

Creamy Tomato Soup

This rich, comforting soup goes perfectly with a grilled cheese sandwich or grilled fish. Fresh tomatoes contain lycopene, an antioxidant with cancer-fighting properties.

 PROGRAM
Pressure Cook

 PRESSURE
High

RELEASE
Natural/Quick

12 organic plum tomatoes

1 tbsp olive oil

2 cups **From-Scratch Chicken Stock (see p100)** or low-sodium chicken stock

1 clove garlic

½ tsp kosher salt

¼ tsp freshly ground black pepper

¼ cup half & half

1 cup fresh basil leaves

1. Combine the tomatoes, olive oil, chicken stock, garlic clove, kosher salt, and pepper in the inner pot.

2. Cover, lock the lid, and flip the steam release handle to the sealing position. Select **Pressure Cook (High)**, and set the cook time for **8 minutes**. When the cook time is complete, allow the pressure to release naturally for 10 minutes, and then quick release the remaining pressure.

3. Remove the lid, and add the half & half and basil. Using an immersion blender, purée the ingredients until a smooth consistency is achieved and no lumps remain.

4. Ladle the soup into serving bowls. Serve hot.

Make this vegan by substituting ½ cup raw, soaked cashews for the cream.

NUTRITION PER SERVING

Total fat **9g**	Cholesterol **20mg**	Carbohydrates **8g**	Sugars **5g**
Saturated fat **4g**	Sodium **298mg**	Dietary fiber **2g**	Protein **4g**

Spicy Lemon-Chive Mussels

Mussels contain inflammation-fighting omega-3 fats, plus other important nutrients. This lighter version features healthy fats from plant-based oils.

274 CALORIES PER SERVING

SERVES **4**
SERVING SIZE **½ lb (225g)**
PREP TIME **10 mins**
COOK TIME **5 mins**
TOTAL TIME **25 mins**

 PROGRAM
Sauté/Pressure Cook

 PRESSURE
Low

RELEASE
Quick

1. Inspect the mussels, discarding any with open shells. Debeard the mussels, and then use a stiff scrub brush to thoroughly scrub each mussel. Rinse and drain.

2. Select **Sauté**, and combine the vegetable oil spread, olive oil, garlic, shallot, red pepper flakes, kosher salt, lemon zest, and lemon juice in the inner pot. Sauté for 2 minutes.

3. Add the wine and mussels to the pot. Using a large spoon, toss to thoroughly coat the mussels in the sauce.

4. Cover, lock the lid, and flip the steam release handle to the sealing position. Select **Pressure Cook (Low)**, and set the cook time for **3 minutes**. When the cook time is complete, quick release the pressure.

5. Remove the lid, transfer the mussels and broth to serving bowls, and sprinkle the chives over top. Serve hot.

2lbs (1kg) fresh mussels
2 tbsp vegetable oil spread
1 tbsp olive oil
2 cloves garlic, thinly sliced
1 shallot, thinly sliced
½ tsp red pepper flakes
½ tsp kosher salt
Zest and juice of 1 lemon
½ cup dry white wine
3 tbsp chopped fresh chives

Serve with slices of toasted whole grain bread to sop up the lemony sauce.

NUTRITION PER SERVING

Total fat **11g**	Cholesterol **64mg**	Carbohydrates **12g**	Sugars **1g**
Saturated fat **2g**	Sodium **612mg**	Dietary fiber **1g**	Protein **27g**

Tex-Mex Chicken Soup

This zesty take on traditional chicken soup is fiery yet flavorful, with plenty of protein from tender chicken, and fiber from vegetables and black beans.

PROGRAM
Sauté/Pressure Cook

PRESSURE
High

RELEASE
Quick

1. Select **Sauté**, and add the olive oil to the inner pot. Add the onion, bell pepper, and poblano pepper, and sauté for 2–3 minutes, or until the onions become soft and translucent.

2. Add the chicken thighs, kosher salt, cayenne pepper, diced tomatoes, and chicken stock to the pot.

3. Cover, lock the lid, and flip the steam release handle to the sealing position. Select **Pressure Cook (High)**, and set the cook time for **12 minutes**. When the cook time is complete, quick release the pressure.

4. Transfer the cooked chicken to a medium bowl and use forks to shred. Return the shredded chicken to the pot, and add the corn and black beans. Stir, and then leave in the pot for 5 minutes to allow the beans and corn to heat through.

5. Ladle the soup into serving bowls, and top each serving with cilantro leaves and a squeeze of fresh lime juice. Serve hot.

1 tbsp olive oil

½ cup chopped yellow onion

1 red bell pepper, seeded and diced

1 poblano pepper, seeded and diced

12oz (340g) boneless, skinless chicken thighs (about 3)

½ tsp kosher salt

¼ tsp cayenne pepper

10oz (285g) can diced tomatoes with green chiles

3 cups **From-Scratch Chicken Stock (see p100)** or low-sodium chicken stock

1 cup frozen corn kernels

1½ cups canned black beans, rinsed and drained

1 cup fresh cilantro leaves

Lime wedges for serving

Dial down the heat by using regular diced tomatoes, and adding a dollop of Greek yogurt.

NUTRITION PER SERVING

Total fat **4g**	Cholesterol **37mg**	Carbohydrates **14g**	Sugars **5g**
Saturated fat **1g**	Sodium **350mg**	Dietary fiber **5g**	Protein **14g**

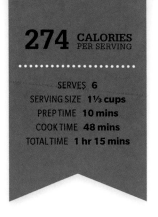

274 CALORIES PER SERVING

SERVES **6**
SERVING SIZE **1⅓ cups**
PREP TIME **10 mins**
COOK TIME **48 mins**
TOTAL TIME **1 hr 15 mins**

Game Day Chili

Watching sporting events is a year-round activity in my house, and cozy bowls of this delectable chili are a must-have part of the festivities.

 PROGRAM
Sauté/Pressure Cook

PRESSURE
High

RELEASE
Natural

1lb (450g) 90% lean ground beef

1 cup chopped onion

1 clove garlic, finely chopped

1½ tsp chili powder

½ tsp ground cumin

1 green bell pepper, seeded and diced

2 tbsp lightly packed light brown sugar

28oz (800g) can crushed tomatoes

15oz (420g) can black beans, rinsed and drained

15oz (420g) can red kidney beans, rinsed and drained

½ tsp kosher salt

4oz (120ml) light beer (optional)

1. Select **Sauté**, and add the ground beef to the inner pot. Brown for 5 minutes, and then carefully remove the inner pot and drain off any rendered fat. Return the inner pot to the base.

2. Add the onion and garlic and sauté for an additional 2–3 minutes, or until the garlic becomes fragrant and the onions become soft and translucent.

3. Add the chili powder and cumin, followed by the bell pepper, brown sugar, tomatoes, black beans, kidney beans, kosher salt, and beer (if using). Stir well.

4. Cover, lock the lid, and flip the steam release handle to the sealing position. Select **Pressure Cook (High)**, and set the cook time for **18 minutes**. When the cook time is complete, allow the pressure to release naturally (about 20 minutes).

5. Remove the lid, and ladle the chili into serving bowls. Serve hot.

Top with fresh cilantro, plain Greek yogurt, shredded low-fat cheese, or tortilla chips.

NUTRITION PER SERVING

Total fat **8g**	Cholesterol **46mg**	Carbohydrates **29g**	Sugars **10g**
Saturated fat **3g**	Sodium **516mg**	Dietary fiber **8g**	Protein **23g**

Butternut Squash Soup

This cozy, made-from-scratch soup is deliciously simple, and made with only a few ingredients. It's very low in calories, but extremely satisfying.

113 CALORIES PER SERVING

SERVES **4**
SERVING SIZE **1 cup**
PREP TIME **10 mins**
COOK TIME **8 mins**
TOTAL TIME **30 mins**

PROGRAM
Pressure Cook

PRESSURE
High

RELEASE
Quick

1. Add the squash, chicken stock, marinara sauce, kosher salt, and pepper to the inner pot. Stir well to combine.

2. Cover, lock the lid, and flip the steam release handle to the sealing position. Select **Pressure Cook (High)**, and set the cook time for **8 minutes**. When the cook time is complete, quick release the pressure.

3. Remove the lid, and add the heavy cream (if using). Using an immersion blender, purée the soup in the pot until a smooth, creamy consistency is achieved. Alternately, allow the soup to cool slightly, and then carefully transfer to a blender and blend on high until the desired consistency is achieved. (Use caution and work in smaller batches when blending, as the steam can cause the lid to explode from the blender.)

4. Ladle the soup into serving bowls. Serve hot.

4 cups peeled and seeded butternut squash, cut into ¾-inch (2cm) cubes

2 cups **From-Scratch Chicken Stock (see p100)** or low-sodium chicken stock

½ cup marinara sauce

½ tsp kosher salt

¼ tsp freshly ground black pepper

2 tbsp heavy cream (optional)

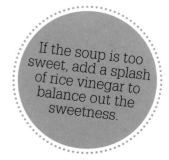

If the soup is too sweet, add a splash of rice vinegar to balance out the sweetness.

NUTRITION PER SERVING

Total fat **3g**	Cholesterol **10mg**	Carbohydrates **20g**	Sugars **6g**
Saturated fat **3g**	Sodium **311mg**	Dietary fiber **3g**	Protein **3g**

143 CALORIES PER SERVING

SERVES **8**
SERVING SIZE **1 cup**
PREP TIME **10 mins**
COOK TIME **20 mins**
TOTAL TIME **50 mins**

2 tsp olive oil

½ cup chopped yellow onion

½ tsp kosher salt

¼ tsp freshly ground
    black pepper

12oz (340g) boneless,
    skinless chicken breasts
    (about 2 to 3 breasts)

1qt (1l) **From-Scratch Chicken
    Stock (see p100)** or
    low-sodium chicken stock

1 bay leaf

1 clove garlic

3 large carrots,
    peeled and chopped

3 large celery stalks,
    peeled and chopped

4oz (110g) dry whole-grain
    egg noodles

Juice of ½ lemon

Just-Like-Mom's Chicken Noodle Soup

This rich, flavorful soup is made with the simplest ingredients: lemon juice adds brightness, while onion, carrots, and celery all add flavor without extra calories.

 PROGRAM
Sauté/Pressure Cook

 PRESSURE
High

RELEASE
Quick

1. Select **Sauté**, and add the olive oil to the inner pot. Add the onion and sauté for 3–5 minutes, or until the onion is soft and translucent. Season with the kosher salt and pepper.

2. Add the chicken breasts to the pot, followed by the chicken stock, bay leaf, and garlic clove.

3. Cover, lock the lid, and flip the steam release handle to the sealing position. Select **Pressure Cook (High)**, and set the cook time for **8 minutes**. When the cook time is complete, quick release the pressure.

4. Remove the lid, and carefully transfer the cooked chicken to a cutting board to cool slightly. When the chicken is cool enough to handle, roughly chop and set aside.

5. Place a fine mesh sieve over a large bowl. Carefully remove the inner pot from the base, strain the broth, and return the broth to the inner pot. Return the inner pot to the base.

6. Select **Sauté**, and add the carrots, celery, and noodles. Allow to simmer for 5 minutes, or until the noodles are tender. Stir in the cooked chicken, and add the lemon juice.

7. Ladle the soup into serving bowls. Serve hot.

NUTRITION PER SERVING

Total fat **3g**	Cholesterol **27mg**	Carbohydrates **14g**	Sugars **2g**
Saturated fat **0g**	Sodium **362mg**	Dietary fiber **3g**	Protein **16g**

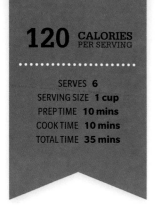

Creamy Cauliflower Cashew Soup

Turmeric adds an earthy flavor, vibrant golden color, and anti-inflammatory benefits to this velvety vegan soup, which features cashews in place of cream.

PROGRAM
Sauté/Pressure Cook

PRESSURE
High

RELEASE
Quick

1 tbsp olive oil, divided

1 clove garlic

1 head cauliflower, trimmed, and chopped into small florets (about 5 cups)

½ cup unsalted cashews

1 tsp ground turmeric

1 tsp kosher salt

½ tsp freshly ground black pepper

3 cups **Vegetable Broth (see p101)** or low-sodium vegetable broth

1. Select **Sauté**, and add 1 teaspoon of the olive oil to the inner pot. Add the garlic clove and sauté for 1–2 minutes, or until the garlic becomes fragrant.

2. Add the cauliflower, cashews, turmeric, kosher salt, and pepper to the pot. Stir well, and then add the vegetable broth.

3. Cover, lock the lid, and flip the steam release handle to the sealing position. Select **Pressure Cook (High)**, and set the cook time for **8 minutes**. When the cook time is complete, quick release the pressure.

4. Remove the lid. Using an immersion blender, purée the soup until a smooth consistency is achieved and no lumps remain. Alternately, allow the soup to cool slightly, transfer to a blender, and blend on high until the desired consistency is achieved. (Use caution and work in smaller batches when blending, as the steam can cause the lid to explode from the blender.)

5. Ladle the soup into serving bowls, and drizzle ⅓ teaspoon olive oil over each serving. Serve hot.

Serve as an appetizer, or as a light lunch along with a hunk of crusty bread.

NUTRITION PER SERVING

Total fat **8g**	Cholesterol **0mg**	Carbohydrates **11g**	Sugars **3g**
Saturated fat **1g**	Sodium **312mg**	Dietary fiber **2g**	Protein **4g**

Kale-Dressed Lentil Soup

Lentils are one of the healthiest foods on the planet, and this light and satisfying soup is made even healthier with a topping of garlicky, sautéed kale.

183 CALORIES PER SERVING

SERVES **6**
SERVING SIZE **1⅓ cups**
PREP TIME **10 mins**
COOK TIME **35 mins**
TOTAL TIME **1 hr**

PROGRAM
Sauté/Pressure Cook

PRESSURE
High

RELEASE
Natural

1. Select **Sauté**, and add 2 teaspoons of the olive oil to the inner pot. Add the kale and garlic, and sauté for 2–3 minutes.

2. Add the balsamic vinegar and sauté for an additional 2–3 minutes, or until the kale is slightly wilted and becomes crispy on the edges. Transfer to a small bowl, and set aside.

3. Add the remaining olive oil to the pot, followed by the scallions, carrot, kosher salt, turmeric, thyme, and cumin. Sauté for 2 minutes.

4. Add the lentils and chicken stock to the pot. Stir well to combine.

5. Cover, lock the lid, and flip the steam release handle to the sealing position. Select **Pressure Cook (High)**, and set the cook time for **12 minutes**. When the cook time is complete, allow the pressure to release naturally (about 15 minutes).

6. Remove the lid and stir. Ladle the soup into serving bowls, and top each serving with the sautéed kale. Serve hot.

1 tbsp olive oil, divided
4 cups chopped kale
1 clove garlic, minced
2 tsp balsamic vinegar
4 scallions, chopped (white and green parts)
1 cup chopped carrot
1 tsp kosher salt
1 tsp ground turmeric
1 tsp dried thyme leaves
½ tsp ground cumin
1 cup green lentils
4 cups **From-Scratch Chicken Stock (see p100)** or low-sodium chicken stock

Make this vegan by substituting low-sodium vegetable broth for the chicken stock.

NUTRITION PER SERVING

Total fat **4g**	Cholesterol **0mg**	Carbohydrates **28g**	Sugars **4g**
Saturated fat **0g**	Sodium **428mg**	Dietary fiber **8g**	Protein **13g**

Broccoli Cheddar Soup

Instead of gobs of high-fat ingredients, this soup features the creamy goodness of winter squash to help thicken the soup, and also add just a hint of sweetness.

139 CALORIES PER SERVING

SERVES **6**
SERVING SIZE **1⅓ cups**
PREP TIME **10 mins**
COOK TIME **11 mins**
TOTAL TIME **30 mins**

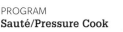
PROGRAM
Sauté/Pressure Cook

PRESSURE
High

RELEASE
Quick

1. Select **Sauté**, and add the olive oil to the inner pot. Add the onion and sauté for 2–3 minutes, or until the onion is soft and translucent.

2. Add the squash, chicken stock, broccoli, garlic powder, kosher salt, and pepper. Stir well.

3. Cover, lock the lid, and flip the steam release handle to the sealing position. Select **Pressure Cook (High)**, and set the cook time for **8 minutes**. When the cook time is complete, quick release the pressure.

4. Remove the lid, and stir in the cheese. Using an immersion blender, purée the soup until a smooth consistency is achieved and no lumps remain. Alternately, allow the soup to cool slightly, carefully transfer to a blender, and blend on high until the desired consistency is achieved. (Use caution and work in smaller batches when blending, as the steam can cause the lid to explode from the blender.)

5. Transfer the soup to serving bowls. Serve hot.

1 tbsp olive oil

1 cup chopped yellow onion

2 cups peeled and cubed butternut squash

4 cups **From-Scratch Chicken Stock (see p100)** or low-sodium chicken stock

3 cups fresh broccoli florets

¼ tsp garlic powder

¾ tsp kosher salt

¼ tsp freshly ground black pepper

¾ cup freshly grated cheddar cheese

You can use pumpkin, or any other type of winter squash, in place of butternut squash.

NUTRITION PER SERVING

Total fat **7g**	Cholesterol **15mg**	Carbohydrates **12g**	Sugars **3g**
Saturated fat **3g**	Sodium **345mg**	Dietary fiber **3g**	Protein **9g**

238 CALORIES
PER SERVING

SERVES **4**
SERVING SIZE **2 cups**
PREP TIME **10 mins**
COOK TIME **45 mins**
TOTAL TIME **1hr 15 mins**

Beef Stew with Root Vegetables

This is quite possibly the easiest—and tastiest—beef stew you'll ever make. Instead of flour, this recipe features gluten-free tapioca to help thicken the sauce.

 PROGRAM
Pressure Cook

 PRESSURE
High

RELEASE
Natural/Quick

1lb (450g) beef brisket, trimmed and cut into 2-inch (5cm) cubes

1 tsp kosher salt

2 tsp dried thyme leaves

½ tsp freshly ground black pepper

½ tsp garlic powder

1 yellow onion, roughly chopped

4 large carrots, peeled and cut into large chunks

2 medium turnips, peeled and cut into large chunks

1 tsp Worcestershire sauce

½ cup low-sodium beef broth

1 tbsp tomato paste

2 tbsp instant tapioca

1. Add the brisket to the inner pot, followed by the kosher salt, thyme, pepper, garlic powder, onion, carrots, turnips, Worcestershire sauce, beef broth, tomato paste, and tapioca. Stir well to combine.

2. Cover, lock the lid, and flip the steam release handle to the sealing position. Select **Pressure Cook (High)**, and set the cook time for **35 minutes**. When the cook time is complete, allow the pressure to release naturally for 10 minutes, and then quick release the remaining pressure.

3. Remove the lid, stir, and allow the stew to cool slightly before ladling into serving bowls. Serve warm.

This is delicious served over a bed of sautéed kale and topped with Sriracha.

NUTRITION PER SERVING

Total fat **9g**	Cholesterol **70mg**	Carbohydrates **14g**	Sugars **6g**
Saturated fat **3g**	Sodium **335mg**	Dietary fiber **4g**	Protein **25g**

Nonni's Pasta e Fagioli

This respectful hack of my grandmother's "macaroni and beans" recipe features escarole, a leafy green veggie that is rich in nutrients and features a bright, peppery edge.

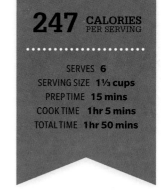

247 CALORIES PER SERVING

SERVES **6**
SERVING SIZE **1⅓ cups**
PREP TIME **15 mins**
COOK TIME **1hr 5 mins**
TOTAL TIME **1hr 50 mins**

 PROGRAM
Pressure Cook/Sauté

 PRESSURE
High

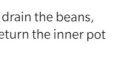 RELEASE
Natural/Quick

1. Add the beans and water to the inner pot.

2. Cover, lock the lid, and flip the steam release handle to the sealing position. Select **Pressure Cook (High)**, and set the cook time for **30 minutes**. When the cook time is complete, allow the pressure to release naturally (about 15 minutes).

3. Carefully remove the inner pot from the base, drain the beans, and then transfer to a large bowl. Set aside. Return the inner pot to the base.

4. Select **Sauté**, and add the olive oil to the pot. Add the garlic, carrot, celery, escarole, kosher salt, and pepper and sauté for 2–3 minutes, or until the vegetables begin to soften and the garlic becomes fragrant.

5. Add the cooked beans to the pot, followed by the chicken stock, and then the ditalini. Using a slotted spoon, press the ingredients down to ensure they are covered in the liquid.

6. Cover, lock the lid, and flip the steam release handle to the sealing position. Select **Pressure Cook (High)**, and set the cook time for **15 minutes**. When the cook time is complete, quick release the pressure.

7. Remove the lid, stir, and then ladle the soup into serving bowls. Sprinkle of a pinch of sea salt and a pinch of red pepper flakes over each serving. Serve hot.

8oz (225g) dry cannellini beans, rinsed and sorted

2 cups water

1 tbsp olive oil

2 cloves garlic, peeled

1 large carrot, peeled and chopped

2 stalks celery, chopped

3 cups chopped escarole

1½ tsp kosher salt

½ tsp freshly ground black pepper

4 cups **From-Scratch Chicken Stock (see p100)** or low-sodium chicken stock

½ cup dry ditalini pasta

Sea salt and red pepper flakes, to serve

Preparing dry beans in the Instant Pot saves time and creates wonderful creaminess.

NUTRITION PER SERVING

Total fat **3g**	Cholesterol **0mg**	Carbohydrates **41g**	Sugars **3g**
Saturated fat **0g**	Sodium **399mg**	Dietary fiber **10g**	Protein **14g**

302 CALORIES PER SERVING

SERVES **6**
SERVING SIZE **2 cups**
PREP TIME **15 mins**
COOK TIME **55 mins**
TOTAL TIME **1hr 25 mins**

Pho Ga

Famous for being a hangover cure, this slurpable Vietnamese soup features high protein chicken, a mineral-rich broth, and anti-inflammatory spices.

PROGRAM
Sauté/Pressure Cook

PRESSURE
High

RELEASE
Natural

1 tbsp canola oil

½ red onion, peeled and cut in half

1-inch (2.5cm) piece fresh ginger root

1 clove garlic

2 tsp coriander seeds

1 cinnamon stick

2 whole star anise

2lbs (1kg) bone-in, skin-on chicken thighs (about 4)

1 tbsp fish sauce

8 cups water

12oz (340g) rice noodles

1 cup fresh cilantro leaves, stems removed

1 cup fresh bean sprouts

1 jalapeño pepper, stem removed and thinly sliced

Sriracha sauce (optional)

Lime wedges, to serve

Using bone-in chicken imparts more minerals and flavor to the broth.

1. Select **Sauté**, and add the canola oil to the inner pot. Heat the oil until it shimmers, and then add the onion. Sauté for 2–3 minutes, or until the onion is lightly browned and slightly translucent. Add the ginger root, garlic, coriander seeds, cinnamon stick, and star anise. Sauté for 1 additional minute, and then add the chicken thighs, fish sauce, and water.

2. Cover, lock the lid, and flip the steam release handle to the sealing position. Select **Pressure Cook (High)**, and set the cook time for **20 minutes**. When the cook time is complete, allow the pressure to release naturally (about 30 minutes).

3. While the broth is cooking, fill a large bowl with warm water and place the rice noodles in the bowl to soften (about 20 minutes).

4. Once the cooking time for the broth is complete, remove the lid and transfer the chicken thighs to a plate to cool slightly. When the thighs are cool enough, remove and discard the skin, shred, and discard the bones.

5. Drain the nodles. Place a fine mesh sieve over a large bowl, carefully remove the inner pot from the base, and strain the broth. Discard the solids and return the strained broth to the inner pot. Select **Sauté**, and bring the broth to a simmer. Add the noodles and simmer for an additional 2–3 minutes. Add the chicken to the pot.

6. Using tongs, transfer the noodles to serving bowls, and then ladle in the broth and chicken. Top each serving with the cilantro leaves, bean sprouts, jalapeño slices, and a dollop of the Sriracha, if using.

NUTRITION PER SERVING

Total fat **3g**	Cholesterol **43mg**	Carbohydrates **48g**	Sugars **3g**
Saturated fat **1g**	Sodium **343mg**	Dietary fiber **1g**	Protein **17g**

SERVES **6**
SERVING SIZE **1½ cups**
PREP TIME **10 mins**
COOK TIME **25 mins**
TOTAL TIME **45 mins**

Creamy Corn Chowder

Serve this refreshing soup as a first course, or with a green salad for a light lunch. This lightened-up version uses milk instead of cream to cut the fat and save calories.

PROGRAM
Sauté/Pressure Cook

PRESSURE
High

RELEASE
Natural/Quick

1 tbsp olive oil

½ medium yellow onion, chopped

1 cup chopped carrot

½ tsp kosher salt

¼ tsp freshly ground black pepper

1 medium russet potato, peeled and diced

2 cups **From-Scratch Chicken Stock (see p100)** or low-sodium chicken stock

1 tbsp cornstarch

2 tbsp water

½ cup whole milk

2 cups frozen corn kernels

2 tbsp chopped fresh chives

1. Select **Sauté**, and add the olive oil to the inner pot. Add the onion, carrot, kosher salt, and pepper, and sauté for 5 minutes, or until the onions are soft and translucent.

2. Add the potato and chicken stock. Stir well. Combine the cornstarch and water in a small bowl. Stir well, and set aside.

3. Cover, lock the lid, and flip the steam release handle to the sealing position. Select **Pressure Cook (High)**, and set the cook time for **5 minutes**. When the cook time is complete, allow the pressure to release naturally for 10 minutes, and then quick release the remaining pressure.

4. Remove the lid, and stir in the milk and corn. Select **Sauté**, bring the ingredients to a simmer, and then add the cornstarch mixture. Stir continuously until the chowder thickens (about 5 minutes).

5. Ladle the chowder into serving bowls and top each serving with chopped chives. Serve hot.

If you prefer to use fresh corn kernels, add them to the pot in step 1.

NUTRITION PER SERVING

Total fat **5g**	Cholesterol **3mg**	Carbohydrates **26g**	Sugars **9g**
Saturated fat **1g**	Sodium **323mg**	Dietary fiber **4g**	Protein **7g**

Kale Soup with Chicken and White Beans

Lean chicken breast and hearty kale are a perfect flavor pairing! Ground chicken breast helps keep the calories under control in this protein-packed soup.

203 CALORIES PER SERVING

SERVES **6**
SERVING SIZE **1⅓ cups**
PREP TIME **10 mins**
COOK TIME **15 mins**
TOTAL TIME **45 mins**

PROGRAM
Sauté/Pressure Cook

PRESSURE
High

RELEASE
Quick

1. Select **Sauté**, and add the olive oil to the inner pot. Add the chicken and sauté for 3–4 minutes, or until the chicken is lightly browned.

2. Add the onion, garlic, carrot, and kale to the pot, and season with the rosemary, kosher salt, and pepper. Sauté for 2 minutes, and then stir in the chicken stock.

3. Cover, lock the lid, and flip the steam release handle to the sealing position. Select **Pressure Cook (High)**, and set the cook time for **8 minutes**. When the cook time is complete, quick release the pressure.

4. Remove the lid, stir in the beans, and then cover for 10 minutes to allow the beans to heat through.

5. Ladle the soup into serving bowls and top each serving with 2 teaspoons of the Parmesan. Serve hot.

2 tsp olive oil
8oz (225g) ground chicken breast
½ cup chopped onion
1 clove garlic, minced
1 cup chopped carrot
6 cups trimmed and chopped kale
2 tsp chopped fresh rosemary
½ tsp kosher salt
¼ tsp freshly ground black pepper
4 cups **From-Scratch Chicken Stock (see p100)** or low-sodium chicken stock
15oz (420g) can cannellini beans, rinsed and drained
4 tbsp grated Parmesan cheese

NUTRITION PER SERVING

Total fat **7g**	Cholesterol **37mg**	Carbohydrates **19g**	Sugars **3g**
Saturated fat **2g**	Sodium **455mg**	Dietary fiber **6g**	Protein **18g**

Vegetable Barley Stew

This light and fabulous stew is heart-healthy and cholesterol-free. It's bursting with hearty pearled barley, and is perfect when you're craving summer vegetables.

212 CALORIES PER SERVING

SERVES **6**
SERVING SIZE **1⅓ cups**
PREP TIME **10 mins**
COOK TIME **21 mins**
TOTAL TIME **45 mins**

PROGRAM
Pressure Cook

PRESSURE
High

RELEASE
Quick

1. Combine the barley, tomatoes, pesto, chicken stock, kosher salt, and pepper in the inner pot.

2. Cover, lock the lid, and flip the steam release handle to the sealing position. Select **Pressure Cook (High)**, and set the cook time for **20 minutes**. When the cook time is complete, quick release the pressure.

3. Remove the lid. Add the zucchini, kale, and green beans to the pot. Stir, and allow to cool for 2 minutes. Cover, lock the lid, and return the steam release handle to the sealing position.

4. Select **Pressure Cook (High)**, and set the cook time for **1 minute**. When the cook time is complete, quick release the pressure.

5. Remove the lid, stir, and then ladle the stew into serving bowls. Top each serving with 1 teaspoon olive oil, chopped basil, and a sprinkle of Parmesan (if using). Serve hot.

1 cup pearled barley, rinsed and drained

14.5oz (410g) can diced tomatoes

1 tbsp pesto sauce

3 cups **From-Scratch Chicken Stock (see p100)** or low-sodium chicken stock

1 tsp kosher salt

½ tsp freshly ground black pepper

1 medium zucchini, chopped

3 cups chopped kale

4oz (110g) fresh green beans, chopped

2 tbsp extra-virgin olive oil

½ cup chopped fresh basil

Grated Parmesan cheese (optional)

NUTRITION PER SERVING

Total fat **6g**	Cholesterol **0mg**	Carbohydrates **36g**	Sugars **5g**
Saturated fat **1g**	Sodium **446mg**	Dietary fiber **8g**	Protein **6g**

From-Scratch Chicken Stock

After you've enjoyed a roasted chicken, save the scraps to make this stellar stock. Making it in the Instant Pot is so much faster than making it on the stovetop!

 PROGRAM
Pressure Cook

 PRESSURE
High

RELEASE
Natural

1 roasted chicken carcass
2 medium carrots, cut in half
½ medium yellow onion
2 celery stalks, cut in half
2 tsp kosher salt
1 tsp black peppercorns
1 bay leaf
1 handful fresh herbs (such as parsley, thyme, rosemary, or tarragon)
8 cups cold water

1. Place the chicken carcass in the inner pot, followed by the carrots, onion, celery, kosher salt, peppercorns, bay leaf, herbs, and water.

2. Cover, lock the lid, and flip the steam release handle to the sealing position. Select **Pressure Cook (High)**, and set the cook time for **1 hour 30 minutes**. When the cook time is complete, allow the pressure to release naturally (about 30 minutes).

3. Place a fine mesh sieve over a large bowl. Allow the stock to cool slightly, and then carefully remove the inner pot from the base and strain the stock through the sieve. Set the stock aside to cool to room temperature. Discard the solids.

4. Once cooled, transfer the stock to sealable 1-quart (1l) glass jars, seal tightly, and place in the refrigerator to chill overnight. Once the stock is chilled, remove the jars from the refrigerator, and skim and discard the layer of fat that forms on the surface. Reseal the jars.

5. Store in the refrigerator for up to one week, or in the freezer for up to six months.

For a milder stock, reduce the cooking time to 30 minutes.

NUTRITION PER SERVING

Total fat **0g**	Cholesterol **0mg**	Carbohydrates **0g**	Sugars **0g**
Saturated fat **0g**	Sodium **287mg**	Dietary fiber **0g**	Protein **5g**

Vegetable Broth

Hold on to all those vegetable scraps and turn them into a savory broth for soups and sauces. This broth is delicious on its own, or used as a base for other recipes.

15 CALORIES PER SERVING

MAKES **2 quarts**
SERVING SIZE **1 cup**
PREP TIME **10 mins**
COOK TIME **1 hr 20 mins**
TOTAL TIME **1 hr 45 mins**

 PROGRAM
Pressure Cook

 PRESSURE
High

 RELEASE
Natural

1. Place the vegetable scraps and herbs in the inner pot, followed by the water.

2. Cover, lock the lid, and flip the steam release handle to the sealing position. Select **Pressure Cook (High)**, and set the cook time for **1 hour**. When the cook time is complete, allow the pressure to release naturally (about 20 minutes).

3. Place a fine mesh sieve over a large bowl. Allow the broth to cool slightly, and then carefully remove the inner pot from the base and strain the stock through the sieve. Set the broth aside to cool to room temperature. Discard the solids.

4. Transfer the strained broth to a sealable glass container. Store in the refrigerator for up to one week, or in the freezer for up to six months.

3 cups vegetable scraps (such as carrots, onion, and celery)

1 cup fresh herbs (such as parsley and thyme)

1½ tsp kosher salt

8 cups cold water

Store vegetable scraps in the freezer until you're ready to make the broth.

NUTRITION PER SERVING

Total fat **0g**	Cholesterol **0mg**	Carbohydrates **4g**	Sugars **1g**
Saturated fat **0g**	Sodium **390mg**	Dietary fiber **0g**	Protein **0g**

Sides & Snacks

Lightened-Up Mac & Cheese

This easy, creamy mac & cheese is ready in 30 minutes in the Instant Pot, and contains a fraction of the fat and calories you'll find in restaurant versions.

PROGRAM
Pressure Cook

PRESSURE
Low

RELEASE
Quick

1 tbsp olive oil

1lb (450g) elbow macaroni

1 tsp kosher salt

4 cups water

5oz (150ml) can 2% evaporated milk

¾ cup grated cheddar cheese

¾ cup grated Monterey Jack cheese

1. Add the olive oil, macaroni, kosher salt, and water to the inner pot. Stir well to combine.

2. Cover, lock the lid, and flip the steam release handle to the sealing position. Select **Pressure Cook (Low)**, and set the cook time for **4 minutes**. When the cook time is complete, quick release the pressure.

3. Remove the lid, carefully remove the inner pot from the base, and transfer to a heat-resistant surface. Add the evaporated milk, cheddar, and Monterey Jack, and stir continuously until the cheese is melted. Set aside to cool and thicken for 10 minutes. Serve warm.

Whole-grain or gluten-free pastas will work equally well for this recipe. Adjust cook times accordingly.

NUTRITION PER SERVING

Total fat **9g**	Cholesterol **20mg**	Carbohydrates **57g**	Sugars **4g**
Saturated fat **4g**	Sodium **314mg**	Dietary fiber **3g**	Protein **15g**

Easy No-Sugar-Added Applesauce

Chop, cook, blend and you have the most delectable applesauce with absolutely no added sugar. Keeping the skins on the apples helps add extra nutrients.

80 CALORIES PER SERVING

MAKES **6 cups**
SERVING SIZE **½ cup**
PREP TIME **10 mins**
COOK TIME **20 mins**
TOTAL TIME **40 mins**

PROGRAM
Pressure Cook

PRESSURE
High

RELEASE
Natural

1. Combine the apples and water in the inner pot.

2. Cover, lock the lid, and flip the steam release handle to the sealing position. Select **Pressure Cook (High)**, and set the cook time for **10 minutes**. When the cook time is complete, allow the pressure to release naturally (about 10 minutes).

3. Remove the lid and add the cinnamon. Using an immersion blender, purée the applesauce until no chunks remain and a smooth consistency is achieved.

4. Transfer to sealable containers and allow to cool completely. Once cooled, seal tightly and store in the refrigerator for up to 1 week, or in the freezer for up to 3 months.

4lbs (1.8kg) apples (Fuji, McIntosh or Gala varieties), cored and roughly chopped
½ cup water
1 tsp ground cinnamon

NUTRITION PER SERVING

Total fat **0g**	Cholesterol **0mg**	Carbohydrates **21g**	Sugars **16g**
Saturated fat **0g**	Sodium **2mg**	Dietary fiber **4g**	Protein **0g**

152 CALORIES PER SERVING

MAKES **1 loaf**
SERVING SIZE **1 slice**
PREP TIME **4 hrs**
COOK TIME **35 mins**
TOTAL TIME **4 hrs 45 mins**

Honey Whole Wheat Bread

In just a few hours you can have a loaf of fresh, crusty bread that contains fewer preservatives than store-bought varieties. And this recipe doesn't require any kneading!

 PROGRAM **Yogurt**

 PRESSURE **none**

RELEASE **none**

2 cups all-purpose flour
1 cup whole-wheat flour
1 tsp kosher salt
2 tsp dry active yeast
1 tbsp honey
1¼ cups warm water, divided

1. Combine the all-purpose flour, whole-wheat flour, salt, and yeast in a large bowl. Whisk until well combined.

2. In a small bowl, combine the honey and 1 cup of the warm water, and stir until the honey is completely dissolved. Add the honey-water mixture to the dry ingredients and mix until the ingredients are well combined. Add the remaining ¼ cup of water to the mixture. Mix until a loose dough ball is formed.

3. Spray a large piece of parchment paper with nonstick cooking spray. Transfer the dough to the parchment paper, place in the pot, and fold the edges of the paper in to fit inside the pot.

4. Cover and lock the lid, but leave the steam release handle in the venting position. Select **Yogurt**, and set the proofing time for **3½ hours**.

5. Once the proofing time is complete, preheat the oven to 450°F (232°C). Remove the lid and turn the dough out onto a generously floured surface. Using clean hands, form the dough into a ball, and then transfer to a fresh sheet of parchment paper.

6. Transfer the dough to a Dutch oven or large cast iron pot. Cover and bake for 30 minutes, and then remove the lid and bake for an additional 5 minutes, or until the top turns golden brown.

7. Transfer the bread to a wire rack to cool for at least 10 minutes before slicing into 10 equal-sized pieces.

Using the yogurt function proofs the dough in just a few hours, instead of overnight.

NUTRITION PER SERVING

Total fat **1g**	Cholesterol **0mg**	Carbohydrates **32g**	Sugars **2g**
Saturated fat **0g**	Sodium **1mg**	Dietary fiber **3g**	Protein **5g**

67 CALORIES
PER SERVING

MAKES **1½ cups**
SERVING SIZE **¼ cup**
PREP TIME **5 mins**
COOK TIME **15 mins**
TOTAL TIME **40 mins**

Homemade Ricotta Cheese

This simple yet versatile recipe will yield the creamiest, dreamiest ricotta cheese you've ever tasted, and it only takes a short time to make in the Instant Pot.

 PROGRAM
Yogurt

 PRESSURE
none

RELEASE
none

5 cups whole milk
¼ cup heavy cream
5 tsp white vinegar
½ tsp kosher salt

1. Combine the milk and cream in the inner pot. Stir gently until the ingredients are well combined.

2. Cover and lock the lid, but leave the steam release handle in the venting position. Select **Yogurt (Boil)**, and wait for the boil cycle to complete. When the cycle is complete, remove the lid, and carefully transfer the inner pot from the base to a heat-resistant surface.

3. Add the vinegar. Stir with a wooden spoon for 3 minutes, or until curds begin to form, and then stir in the kosher salt.

4. Place a fine mesh sieve lined with cheesecloth over a large bowl. Pour the mixture into the sieve and allow the ricotta to drain for 15 minutes.

5. Transfer the drained ricotta to a sealable container and allow to cool completely before transferring to the refrigerator. Refrigerate for up to 5 days.

Reserve the nutrient-rich whey to use in smoothies, or in soups.

NUTRITION PER SERVING

Total fat **4g**	Cholesterol **18mg**	Carbohydrates **2g**	Sugars **1g**
Saturated fat **3g**	Sodium **900mg**	Dietary fiber **0g**	Protein **5g**

Herbed Brown Rice

The Instant Pot also works as a dynamite rice cooker!
The nutty goodness of this delicate brown rice delivers
more nutritional punch than white rice.

129 CALORIES PER SERVING

SERVES **10**
SERVING SIZE **½ cup**
PREP TIME **5 mins**
COOK TIME **34 mins**
TOTAL TIME **45 mins**

 PROGRAM
Pressure Cook

 PRESSURE
High

 RELEASE
Natural

1. Add the rice, salt, and water to the inner pot. Cover, lock the lid, and flip the steam release handle to the sealing position.

2. Select **Pressure Cook (High)**, and set the cook time for **22 minutes**. When the cook time is complete, allow the pressure to release naturally (about 12 minutes).

3. Remove the lid and transfer to a serving bowl. Add the herbs and lemon zest, mix well, and then fluff with a fork. Serve hot.

2 cups long grain brown rice, rinsed and drained

1 tsp kosher salt

2¼ cups water

½ cup chopped fresh herbs (parsley and tarragon recommended)

2 tsp freshly grated lemon zest

NUTRITION PER SERVING

Total fat **1g**	Cholesterol **0mg**	Carbohydrates **26g**	Sugars **0g**
Saturated fat **0g**	Sodium **114mg**	Dietary fiber **2g**	Protein **2g**

Loaded Sweet Potato Skins

These super healthy skins are loaded with vitamins and minerals, feature vibrant colors and flavors, and have a fraction of the fat and calories of traditional skins.

195 CALORIES PER SERVING

MAKES **6**
SERVING SIZE **1**
PREP TIME **15 mins**
COOK TIME **30 mins**
TOTAL TIME **1 hr 10 mins**

 PROGRAM
Pressure Cook

 PRESSURE
High

RELEASE
Quick

1. Place the steam rack in the inner pot. Add 1 cup water, and then add the beets.

2. Cover, lock the lid, and flip the steam release handle to the sealing position. Select **Pressure Cook (High)**, and set the cook time for **15 minutes**. When the cook time is complete, quick release the pressure.

3. Transfer the cooked beets to a cutting board and allow to cool slightly. Once the beets are cool enough to handle, peel, dice, and set aside.

4. Carefully remove the inner pot from the base, drain, and wipe clean Return the inner pot to the base, place the steam rack back in the pot, and add 1 cup water. Using a fork, pierce the skin of each sweet potato, and then place the potatoes in the pot.

5. Cover, lock the lid, and flip the steam release handle to the sealing position. Select **Pressure Cook (High)**, and set the cook time for **15 minutes**. When the cook time is complete, quick release the pressure.

6. Transfer the cooked sweet potatoes to a cutting board and allow to cool slightly. Once the potatoes are cool enough to handle, cut each in half lengthwise and use a spoon to scoop out the flesh. Transfer the skins to a serving platter, and set aside. Transfer the flesh to medium bowl. Add the Greek yogurt, kosher salt, red pepper flakes, and spinach to the bowl. Mix well.

7. Fill each skin with equal amounts of the filling, then top each with the chopped beets and a spoonful of the feta. Serve warm.

3 small beets
3 medium sweet potatoes
2 tbsp **Homemade Greek Yogurt (see p33)** or low-fat Greek yogurt
½ tsp kosher salt
Pinch red pepper flakes
2 cups fresh baby spinach
⅓ cup crumbled feta cheese

Top with black beans and serve as a vegetarian main course.

NUTRITION PER SERVING

Total fat **4g**	Cholesterol **15mg**	Carbohydrates **35g**	Sugars **11g**
Saturated fat **3g**	Sodium **408mg**	Dietary fiber **6g**	Protein **7g**

SERVES **6**
SERVING SIZE **¾ cup**
PREP TIME **5 mins**
COOK TIME **12 mins**
TOTAL TIME **22 mins**

Cinnamon Coconut Rice

This fluffy, perfumed rice pairs perfectly with meat, fish, or vegetables. Just the right amount of coconut milk makes this side satisfying, without going overboard on the fat.

 PROGRAM
Rice

 PRESSURE
Low

RELEASE
Quick

1 cup white basmati rice, rinsed and drained
½ cup canned coconut milk
¾ cup water
¼ tsp kosher salt
1 cinnamon stick
1 tbsp finely chopped scallions
1 tbsp sesame seeds

1. Combine the rice, coconut milk, water, kosher salt, and the cinnamon stick in the inner pot.

2. Cover, lock the lid, and flip the steam release handle to the sealing position. Select **Rice (Low)**, and set the cook time for **12 minutes**. When the cook time is complete, quick release the pressure.

3. Remove the lid, discard the cinnamon stick, and transfer to a serving bowl. Fluff with a fork, and top with the scallions and sesame seeds. Serve hot.

NUTRITION PER SERVING

Total fat **7g**	Cholesterol **0mg**	Carbohydrates **42g**	Sugars **0g**
Saturated fat **5g**	Sodium **75mg**	Dietary fiber **1g**	Protein **5g**

Perfect Hard-Cooked Eggs

There's no need to struggle with hard boiling eggs when a quick burst of pressure in the Instant Pot can cook them to perfection every single time.

72 CALORIES PER SERVING

MAKES **12**
SERVING SIZE **1**
PREP TIME **2 mins**
COOK TIME **10 mins**
TOTAL TIME **25 mins**

PROGRAM
Pressure Cook

PRESSURE
High

RELEASE
Quick

1 dozen large eggs

1. Place the steam rack in the inner pot, and add 1 cup water. Gently place the eggs in the pot. Fill a large bowl with ice water.

2. Cover, lock the lid, and flip the steam release handle to the sealing position. Select **Pressure Cook (High)**, and set the cook time for **10 minutes**. When the cook time is complete, quick release the pressure. (For a slightly softer yolk, adjust the pressure level to **Low**).

3. Using tongs, transfer the cooked eggs to the ice bath and allow to cool for 5 minutes. Transfer the cooled eggs to an airtight container, and store in the refrigerator for up to one week.

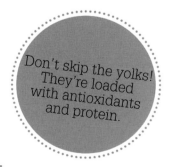

Don't skip the yolks! They're loaded with antioxidants and protein.

NUTRITION PER SERVING

Total fat **5g**	Cholesterol **186mg**	Carbohydrates **0g**	Sugars **0g**
Saturated fat **2g**	Sodium **71mg**	Dietary fiber **0g**	Protein **6g**

SERVES **8**
SERVING SIZE **1 cup**
PREP TIME **10 mins**
COOK TIME **16 mins**
TOTAL TIME **45 mins**

Asian Quinoa Salad

This Asian-inspired salad packs plenty of fiber and protein. The flavors might taste like takeout, but this dish features a whole lot less fat and fewer calories!

PROGRAM	PRESSURE	RELEASE
Pressure Cook	**High**	**Natural**

2 cups quinoa, rinsed and drained

2 cups water

1 tsp kosher salt

2 tsp grated fresh ginger

1 tbsp sesame oil

1 tbsp almond butter

2 tsp reduced-sodium soy sauce

Juice of one lime

1 tbsp honey

1 tbsp rice vinegar

1 cup grated carrot

½ cup shelled edamame

½ cup chopped red bell pepper

½ cup diced cucumber

¾ cup roasted cashews

1. Combine the quinoa, water, and kosher salt in the inner pot.

2. Cover, lock the lid, and flip the steam release handle to the sealing position. Select **Pressure Cook (High)**, and set the cook time for **1 minute**. When the cook time is complete, allow the pressure to release naturally (about 15 minutes).

3. Remove the lid, and transfer the cooked quinoa to a large bowl to cool slightly (about 10 minutes).

4. Make the dressing by combining the ginger, sesame oil, almond butter, soy sauce, lime juice, honey, and rice vinegar in a small bowl. Whisk until well combined.

5. Add the carrot, edamame, bell pepper, cucumber, and cashews to the quinoa. Toss well to combine, and then add the dressing. Toss to coat the ingredients in the dressing.

6. Transfer to serving bowls. Serve warm.

For a burst of heat that adds just a few calories, add 2 teaspoons of Sriracha sauce to the dressing.

NUTRITION PER SERVING

Total fat **12g**	Cholesterol **0mg**	Carbohydrates **37g**	Sugars **4g**
Saturated fat **2g**	Sodium **180mg**	Dietary fiber **4g**	Protein **10g**

121 CALORIES PER SERVING

SERVES **4**
SERVING SIZE **¾ cup**
PREP TIME **10 mins**
COOK TIME **9 mins**
TOTAL TIME **30 mins**

Buttermilk Mashed Potatoes

Potatoes are a nutrition powerhouse! Low-fat buttermilk and light sour cream are the keys to lightening up this warm and comforting side dish.

PROGRAM
Pressure Cook

PRESSURE
High

RELEASE
Quick

1lb (450g) russet potatoes, peeled and diced into 1-inch (2.5cm) cubes
½ tsp kosher salt, divided
¼ cup low-fat buttermilk
2 tbsp light sour cream
1 tbsp vegetable oil spread
2 tbsp chopped fresh chives
Freshly ground black pepper

1. Place the steam rack in the inner pot, and add 1 cup water. Add the potatoes and season with ¼ teaspoon of the kosher salt.

2. Cover, lock the lid, and flip the steam release handle to the sealing position. Select **Pressure Cook (High)**, and set the cook time for **9 minutes**. When the cook time is complete, quick release the pressure.

3. Carefully transfer the potatoes to a large bowl. Add the buttermilk, sour cream, vegetable oil spread, and remaining kosher salt. Using a potato masher, mash the ingredients until a smooth consistency is achieved and no lumps remain.

4. Transfer to a serving bowl. Sprinkle the chives over top, and season with pepper to taste. Serve warm.

NUTRITION PER SERVING

Total fat **4g**	Cholesterol **3mg**	Carbohydrates **19g**	Sugars **3g**
Saturated fat **1g**	Sodium **205mg**	Dietary fiber **3g**	Protein **3g**

Herbed Street Corn

This lighter spin on a classic street snack cuts the fat way back. Corn contains plenty of fiber plus the antioxidant lutein, which helps promote healthy vision.

154 CALORIES PER SERVING

SERVES **4**
SERVING SIZE **1 ear**
PREP TIME **5 mins**
COOK TIME **5 mins**
TOTAL TIME **15 mins**

 PROGRAM
Steam

 PRESSURE
High

 RELEASE
Quick

1. Place the steam rack in the inner pot, and add 1 cup water. Place the corn in the pot.

2. Cover, lock the lid, and flip the steam release handle to the sealing position. Select **Steam (High)**, adjust the mode to **Normal**, and set the cook time for **5 minutes**.

3. While the corn is cooking, make the sauce by combining the Greek yogurt, mayonnaise, kosher salt, pepper, and parsley in a small bowl. Stir well to combine.

4. When the cook time for the corn is complete, quick release the pressure, remove the lid, and transfer the corn to a serving plate.

5. Top each ear with 2 teaspoons of the sauce, and sprinkle the feta over top. Serve hot.

4 medium ears corn, shucked
4 tsp nonfat Greek yogurt
2 tsp mayonnaise
¼ tsp kosher salt
¼ tsp Freshly ground black pepper
2 tbsp chopped fresh parsley
¼ cup crumbled feta cheese

NUTRITION PER SERVING

Total fat **4g**	Cholesterol **5mg**	Carbohydrates **30g**	Sugars **5g**
Saturated fat **1g**	Sodium **136mg**	Dietary fiber **4g**	Protein **5g**

Can't-Be-Beet Salad

Simply dressed, adorned with salty cheese, and speckled with fresh herbs—this is the best beet salad ever! A quick cook in the Instant Pot helps retain key nutrients.

124 CALORIES PER SERVING

SERVES **6**
SERVING SIZE **1 cup**
PREP TIME **10 mins**
COOK TIME **27 mins**
TOTAL TIME **55 mins**

 PROGRAM
Pressure Cook

 PRESSURE
High

RELEASE
Natural

1. Place the steam rack in the inner pot, and add 1½ cups water. Add the beets.

2. Cover, lock the lid, and flip the steam release handle to the sealing position. Select **Pressure Cook (High)**, and set the cook time for **15 minutes**. When the cook time is complete, allow the pressure to release naturally (about 12 minutes).

3. Using tongs, carefully transfer the beets to a plate and allow to cool slightly. Once the beets are cool enough to handle, gently peel away the skins, slice, and chop.

4. Transfer the beets to a large bowl. Add the olive oil, lemon juice, kosher salt, and pepper. Toss gently.

5. Transfer to serving plates, and sprinkle the feta and chives over top of each serving. Serve at room temperature, or serve chilled. (Store in a sealable container in the refrigerator for up to 5 days.)

2lbs (1kg) beets (about 5 medium beets), washed and patted dry, ends trimmed
2 tbsp olive oil
Juice ½ lemon
½ tsp kosher salt
¼ tsp freshly ground black pepper
¼ cup crumbled feta cheese
2 tbsp chopped fresh chives

Beets are rich in natural nitrates that promote circulation and help lower blood pressure.

NUTRITION PER SERVING

Total fat **6g**	Cholesterol **6mg**	Carbohydrates **15g**	Sugars **11g**
Saturated fat **2g**	Sodium **269mg**	Dietary fiber **4g**	Protein **3g**

Less-Salt BBQ Baked Beans

These delicious beans are ready in about the same amount of time it takes to heat a pan of beans on the stovetop, and the sodium is slashed by more than 400mg per serving.

PROGRAM
Pressure Cook

PRESSURE
Low

RELEASE
Quick

2 tbsp maple syrup

2 tbsp molasses

1 tsp Dijon mustard

¼ cup ketchup

½ tsp garlic powder

2 x 15oz (420g) cans cannellini or pinto beans, rinsed and drained

¼ cup water

1. Make the sauce by combining the maple syrup, molasses, Dijon mustard, ketchup, and garlic powder in a small bowl. Mix well.

2. Combine the beans and water in the inner pot, and add the sauce. Mix well to combine.

3. Cover, lock the lid, and flip the steam release handle to the sealing position. Select **Pressure Cook (Low)**, and set the cook time for **4 minutes**. When the cook time is complete, quick release the pressure.

4. Remove the lid, stir, and transfer to a serving bowl. Serve hot.

NUTRITION PER SERVING

Total fat **1g**	Cholesterol **0mg**	Carbohydrates **30g**	Sugars **12g**
Saturated fat **0g**	Sodium **154mg**	Dietary fiber **5g**	Protein **6g**

Cran-Mango Chutney

This sweet and sour condiment is fat-free and will give a flavor boost to everything from curries to sandwiches. Mangoes and cranberries are both loaded with vitamin C.

40 CALORIES PER SERVING

MAKES **1½ cups**
SERVING SIZE **1 tbsp**
PREP TIME **10 mins**
COOK TIME **32 mins**
TOTAL TIME **55 mins**

PROGRAM
Sauté/Pressure Cook

PRESSURE
High

RELEASE
Natural

1. Select **Sauté**, and add the canola oil to the inner pot. Add the onion, garlic, and ginger, and sauté for 2 minutes.

2. Add the bell pepper, mango, cranberries, and kosher salt. Stir, and then add the vinegar, brown sugar, mustard seeds, and chili paste. Continue to stir until the ingredients are well combined.

3. Cover, lock the lid, and flip the steam release handle to the sealing position. Select **Pressure Cook (High)**, and set the cook time for **10 minutes**. When the cook time is complete, allow the pressure to release naturally (about 15 minutes).

4. Remove the lid, and stir. Select **Sauté**, and allow the chutney to simmer for 5 minutes, or until a jam-like consistency is achieved, and then press **Cancel** to turn off the heat.

5. Transfer to a sealable glass container and allow to cool to room temperature. Once cooled, seal, and transfer to the refrigerator. Store in the refrigerator for up to 2 weeks.

1 tsp canola oil
¼ cup finely chopped yellow onion
1 clove garlic, minced
2 tsp finely chopped ginger root
½ red bell pepper, finely chopped
3 cups frozen mango chunks
½ cup no-sugar-added dried cranberries
¼ tsp kosher salt
½ cup rice vinegar
½ cup light brown sugar, lightly packed
1 tsp brown mustard seeds
2 tsp Sambal Oelek chili paste

NUTRITION PER SERVING

Total fat **0g**	Cholesterol **0mg**	Carbohydrates **10g**	Sugars **9g**
Saturated fat **0g**	Sodium **17mg**	Dietary fiber **0g**	Protein **0g**

187 CALORIES PER SERVING

SERVES **6**
SERVING SIZE **1 cup**
PREP TIME **5 mins**
COOK TIME **34 mins**
TOTAL TIME **50 mins**

Mexican Cheesy Rice

Cheesy rice is quite possibly my kids' favorite side. This healthier version features turmeric and coriander, which both fight inflammation and promote healthy digestion.

 PROGRAM
Pressure Cook

 PRESSURE
High

RELEASE
Natural

2 cups long grain brown rice, rinsed and drained

1¼ tsp kosher salt, divided

2¼ cups water

¼ tsp garlic powder

¼ tsp ground turmeric

¼ tsp ground coriander

1 tbsp canola oil

1 cup shredded Monterey Jack cheese

Juice of ½ lemon

1 cup frozen peas

1. Combine the rice, 1 teaspoon of the kosher salt, and water in the inner pot.

2. Cover, lock the lid, and flip the steam release handle to the sealing position. Select **Pressure Cook (High)**, and set the cook time for **22 minutes**.

3. While the rice is cooking, make the spice mix by combining the garlic powder, turmeric, remaining kosher salt, and coriander in a small bowl. Mix well.

4. When the cook time for the rice is complete, allow the pressure to release naturally (about 12 minutes). Remove the lid, add the spice mix, canola oil, Monterey Jack, lemon juice, and peas. Stir until the cheese is melted, and the ingredients are well incorporated.

5. Transfer to a serving bowl. Serve warm.

This version contains less salt than boxed versions, and contains no preservatives.

NUTRITION PER SERVING

Total fat **6g**	Cholesterol **17mg**	Carbohydrates **25g**	Sugars **1g**
Saturated fat **3g**	Sodium **271mg**	Dietary fiber **2g**	Protein **7g**

Low-Carb Mashed Cauliflower

This lighter, lower carb alternative to mashed potatoes is every bit as savory and satisfying, and features protein-packed Greek yogurt in place of sour cream.

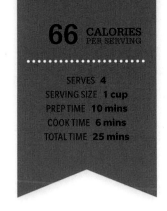

66 CALORIES PER SERVING

SERVES **4**
SERVING SIZE **1 cup**
PREP TIME **10 mins**
COOK TIME **6 mins**
TOTAL TIME **25 mins**

PROGRAM
Steam/Sauté

PRESSURE
High

RELEASE
Quick

1. Place the steam rack in the inner pot. Add the cauliflower and 1 cup water.

2. Cover, lock the lid, and flip the steam release handle to the sealing position. Select **Steam (High)**, and set the cook time for **4 minutes**. When the cook time is complete, quick release the pressure.

3. Remove the lid, and transfer the cauliflower to a large bowl. Carefully remove the inner pot from the base, drain, and return to the base.

4. Select **Sauté**, and add the vegetable oil spread, cooked cauliflower, Greek yogurt, kosher salt, and pepper to the inner pot. Sauté for 2 minutes.

5. Using a potato masher, mash the ingredients until a smooth consistency is achieved, and no large lumps remain.

6. Transfer to a serving bowl. Serve warm.

1 head cauliflower, trimmed and chopped into small florets (about 5 cups)
1 tbsp vegetable oil spread
2 tbsp plain 2% Greek yogurt
¾ tsp kosher salt
¼ tsp freshly ground black pepper

Cruciferous vegetables like cauliflower contain cancer-fighting properties.

NUTRITION PER SERVING

Total fat **3g**	Cholesterol **0mg**	Carbohydrates **7g**	Sugars **3g**
Saturated fat **1g**	Sodium **278mg**	Dietary fiber **3g**	Protein **3g**

253 CALORIES
PER SERVING

....

SERVES **6**
SERVING SIZE **¾ cup**
PREP TIME **5 mins**
COOK TIME **15 mins**
TOTAL TIME **35 mins**

Mediterranean Wild Rice Salad

Wild rice is high in protein and an antioxidant powerhouse. The earthiness of this rice is balanced by flavors of lemon, pomegranate, and tangy goat cheese.

 PROGRAM
Pressure Cook

 PRESSURE
High

 RELEASE
Natural/Quick

2 cups wild rice, rinsed and drained

2¼ cups water

1 tsp kosher salt

2 tbsp olive oil

2 tbsp freshly squeezed lemon juice

2 tsp lemon zest

½ cup pomegranate arils

½ cup chopped celery

½ cup shelled pistachios, roughly chopped

½ cup crumbled goat cheese

1. Combine the rice, water, and kosher salt in the inner pot.

2. Cover, lock the lid, and flip the steam release handle to the sealing position. Select **Pressure Cook (High)**, and set the cook time for **10 minutes**. When the cook time is complete, allow the pressure to release naturally for 5 minutes, and then quick release the remaining pressure.

3. Remove the lid. Transfer the cooked rice to a large bowl to cool slightly.

4. Add the olive oil, lemon juice, lemon zest, pomegranate arils, celery, and pistachios to the bowl. Toss gently.

5. Transfer to serving bowls, and sprinkle the goat cheese over top of each serving. Serve warm.

NUTRITION PER SERVING

Total fat **10g**	Cholesterol **6mg**	Carbohydrates **35g**	Sugars **3g**
Saturated fat **2g**	Sodium **178mg**	Dietary fiber **4g**	Protein **9g**

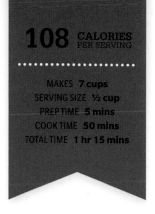

108 CALORIES
PER SERVING

· · · · · · · · · · · · · · · · · · · ·

MAKES **7 cups**
SERVING SIZE **½ cup**
PREP TIME **5 mins**
COOK TIME **50 mins**
TOTAL TIME **1 hr 15 mins**

1lb (450g) dried black beans,
rinsed, drained, and sorted
2 tsp kosher salt
1 dried bay leaf
4 cups water

Perfect Black Beans

These creamy, tender beans are a stellar addition to soups or dips, and also are delicious on their own. They contain a fraction of the sodium found in canned black beans.

· ·

 PROGRAM
Pressure Cook

PRESSURE
High

RELEASE
Natural

1. Combine the beans, kosher salt, bay leaf, and water in the inner pot.

2. Cover, lock the lid, and flip the steam release handle to the sealing position. Select **Pressure Cook (High)**, and set the cook time for **30 minutes**. When the cook time is complete, allow the pressure to release naturally (about 20 minutes).

3. Remove the lid, stir, and check for doneness. (The beans should be tender, but not mushy.) Carefully remove the inner pot from the base, and drain any remaining liquid.

4. Transfer to a serving bowl. Serve hot. Alternately, transfer the cooled beans to an airtight container and store in the refrigerator for up to one week, or in the freezer for up to 3 months.

NUTRITION PER SERVING

| Total fat **0g** | Cholesterol **0mg** | Carbohydrates **21g** | Sugars **5g** |
| Saturated fat **0g** | Sodium **150mg** | Dietary fiber **8g** | Protein **7g** |

Salsa Verde

Bright and tangy tomatillos are packed with fiber, vitamins, minerals and antioxidants. Use this bold, low-calorie, low-fat salsa as a condiment on any Mexican dish.

33 CALORIES PER SERVING

MAKES **3 cups**
SERVING SIZE **¾ cup**
PREP TIME **10 mins**
COOK TIME **5 mins**
TOTAL TIME **25 mins**

 PROGRAM
Sauté/Pressure Cook

 PRESSURE
High

 RELEASE
Quick

1. Select **Sauté**, and add the olive oil to the inner pot. Add the garlic, onion, tomatillos, jalapeño, and kosher salt. Sauté for 2 minutes, or until liquid begins to appear at the bottom of the pot.

2. Cover, lock the lid, and flip the steam release handle to the sealing position. Select **Pressure Cook (High)**, and set the cook time for **3 minutes**. When the cook time is complete, quick release the pressure.

3. Remove the lid, and add the lime juice and cilantro. Using an immersion blender, purée the ingredients until a smooth texture is achieved and no lumps remain. Alternately, transfer the ingredients to a food processer or blender, and pulse until the desired consistency is achieved.

4. Transfer the cooled salsa to a sealable container. Store in the refrigerator for up to one week, or in the freezer for up to 3 months. Serve chilled.

1 tbsp olive oil

1 clove garlic, sliced

½ white onion, roughly chopped

1½lbs (680g) tomatillos, husks removed, and quartered

1 jalapeño pepper, stem removed, and roughly chopped

2 tsp kosher salt

Juice of one lime

1½ cups fresh cilantro

NUTRITION PER SERVING

Total fat **2g**	Cholesterol **0mg**	Carbohydrates **5g**	Sugars **3g**
Saturated fat **0g**	Sodium **132mg**	Dietary fiber **1g**	Protein **1g**

Baked Spaghetti Squash

This low-carb pasta alternative saves 150 calories per serving compared to traditional pasta, and it's loaded with vitamins. You won't miss the pasta one bit!

204 CALORIES PER SERVING

SERVES **4**
SERVING SIZE **2 cups**
PREP TIME **10 mins**
COOK TIME **25 mins**
TOTAL TIME **50 mins**

 PROGRAM
Sauté/Pressure Cook

 PRESSURE
High

RELEASE
Quick

1. Select **Sauté**, and add the olive oil to the inner pot. Add the garlic, onion, fennel seed, salt, and pepper. Sauté for 2 minutes, and then add the tomatoes. Cook for an additional 3 minutes, stirring frequently, and then press **Cancel** to turn off the heat. Transfer the marinara to a large bowl and set aside.

2. Carefully clean the inner pot, return it to the base, and place the steam rack in the pot. Preheat the broiler to high.

3. Using a fork, pierce all sides of the squash. Place it in the inner pot, along with 1 cup water.

4. Cover, lock the lid, and flip the steam release handle to the sealing position. Select **Pressure Cook (High)**, and set the cook time for **15 minutes**. When the cook time is complete, quick release the pressure.

5. Transfer the steamed squash to a cutting board and allow to cool slighly. When the squash is cool enough to handle, cut it in half lengthwise, and use a spoon to scoop out the seeds. Using a fork, shred the squash into "spaghetti." Transfer the squash to a large bowl, and reserve the shells.

6. Add the marinara sauce and mozzarella to the squash. Mix well.

7. Transfer the shells to a large baking sheet. Divide the filling across each shell, and sprinkle ½ teaspoon Italian seasoning over top of each shell. Broil for 5 minutes, or until the cheese is melted and bubbly.

8. Transfer the halves to a serving plate. Serve hot from the shells.

1 medium spaghetti squash
1 cup part-skim shredded mozzarella cheese
1 tsp Italian seasoning

For the marinara:
1 tbsp olive oil
1 clove garlic, minced
½ small yellow onion, finely chopped
½ tsp ground fennel seed
¼ tsp kosher salt
¼ tsp freshly ground black pepper
2½ cups canned crushed tomatoes

If you prefer some heat, sprinkle a pinch of red pepper flakes over each half.

NUTRITION PER SERVING

Total fat **7g**	Cholesterol **15mg**	Carbohydrates **27g**	Sugars **12g**
Saturated fat **3g**	Sodium **395mg**	Dietary fiber **5g**	Protein **10g**

Red Lentil and White Rice Pilaf

This earthy, mild side dish is perfect on its own, or added to stir-frys, burritos, or chili. Lentils contain more than twice the protein and six times the fiber of white rice.

PROGRAM
Sauté/Rice

PRESSURE
Low

RELEASE
Quick

2 tsp olive oil

¼ cup finely chopped yellow onion

1 tsp kosher salt

¼ tsp freshly ground black pepper

1 cup red lentils, rinsed and drained

1 cup long grain white rice, rinsed and drained

2 cups water

1. Select **Sauté**, and add the olive oil to the inner pot. Add the onion, kosher salt, and pepper, and sauté for 2 minutes, or until the onion becomes soft and translucent.

2. Add the lentils, rice, and water to the pot. Stir well.

3. Cover, lock the lid, and flip the steam release handle to the sealing position. Select **Rice (Less)**, and set the cook time for **8 minutes**. When the cook time is complete, quick release the pressure.

4. Remove the lid, transfer to a serving bowl, and fluff with a fork. Serve hot.

Boost the flavor with fresh parsley, chopped scallion, or a few pinches of red pepper flakes.

NUTRITION PER SERVING

Total fat **3g**	Cholesterol **0mg**	Carbohydrates **42g**	Sugars **2g**
Saturated fat **0g**	Sodium **190mg**	Dietary fiber **6g**	Protein **11g**

Chili Queso

Store-bought queso typically is loaded with thickeners, oils, and other artificial ingredients. Make your own in the Instant Pot using nothing but whole food ingredients!

151 CALORIES PER SERVING

MAKES **2 cups**
SERVING SIZE **¼ cup**
PREP TIME **10 mins**
COOK TIME **8 mins**
TOTAL TIME **25 mins**

 PROGRAM
Sauté/Pressure Cook

 PRESSURE
High

RELEASE
Quick

1. In a medium bowl, combine the pepper jack, cheddar, and cornstarch. Toss well to combine, and set aside.

2. Select **Sauté**, and add the olive oil to the inner pot. Add the shallot, poblano, jalapeño, and kosher salt, and sauté for 2–3 minutes. Add the chicken stock and tomatoes. Stir well.

3. Cover, lock the lid, and flip the steam release handle to the sealing position. Select **Pressure Cook (High)**, and set the cook time for **5 minutes**. When the cook time is complete, quick release the pressure.

4. Remove the lid, and add the cheese mixture. Whisk continuously until the cheese is completely melted, and a smooth consistency is achieved.

5. Transfer to a serving bowl, and add the hot sauce (if using). Serve hot.

4oz (110g) pepper jack cheese, shredded

4oz (110g) cheddar cheese, shredded

1 tbsp cornstarch

1 tbsp olive oil

2 tbsp chopped shallot

1 small poblano pepper, stem removed, and finely chopped

1 jalapeño pepper, stem removed, and finely chopped

½ tsp kosher salt

½ cup **From-Scratch Chicken Stock (see p100)** or low-sodium chicken stock

½ cup canned diced tomatoes with green chiles

5 dashes hot sauce (optional)

For a different flavor, substitute any light beer for the chicken stock.

NUTRITION PER SERVING

Total fat **12g**	Cholesterol **30mg**	Carbohydrates **3g**	Sugars **1g**
Saturated fat **7g**	Sodium **256mg**	Dietary fiber **3g**	Protein **6g**

Mediterranean Farro Salad

Farro is an ancient grain with a beautifully nutty flavor and a chewy texture. It's protein rich, and also helps promote heart health and healthy weight loss.

	PROGRAM **Pressure Cook**		PRESSURE **High**		RELEASE **Quick**

2 cups whole-grain farro, rinsed and drained

2 cups water

1¼ tsp kosher salt, divided

2 tbsp olive oil

2 tbsp balsamic vinegar

15oz (420g) can cannellini beans, rinsed and drained

¼ cup chopped packed-in-oil sun-dried tomatoes, drained

¼ cup thinly sliced red onion

½ cup crumbled feta cheese

¼ cup chopped kalamata olives

3 cups fresh baby spinach

½ tsp freshly ground black pepper

1. Combine the farro, water, and 1 tsp of the kosher salt in the inner pot. Stir well.

2. Cover, lock the lid, and flip the steam release handle to the sealing position. Select **Pressure Cook (High)**, and set the cook time for **25 minutes**. When the cook time is complete, quick release the pressure.

3. Remove the lid. Transfer the farro to a large colander. Rinse, drain, and then transfer to a large bowl.

4. Add the olive oil, pepper, vinegar, beans, sun-dried tomatoes, onion, feta, olives, spinach, pepper, and remaining kosher salt to the bowl. Toss gently.

5. Transfer to a serving bowl and allow to cool to room temperature before serving.

NUTRITION PER SERVING

Total fat **9g**	Cholesterol **8mg**	Carbohydrates **37g**	Sugars **3g**
Saturated fat **2g**	Sodium **249mg**	Dietary fiber **5g**	Protein **8g**

138 CALORIES
PER SERVING

SERVES **6**
SERVING SIZE **¾ cup**
PREP TIME **10 mins**
COOK TIME **20 mins**
TOTAL TIME **45 mins**

Pumpkin Sage Stuffing

Stuffing is too delicious to just serve at holiday meals! Instead of using gobs of butter, this version stays moist and flavorful with the help of antioxidant-rich pumpkin purée.

 PROGRAM
Sauté/Pressure Cook

PRESSURE
High

RELEASE
Quick

2 tbsp olive oil

½ large yellow onion, finely chopped

2 tbsp chopped fresh sage

2 tsp chopped fresh thyme

½ tsp kosher salt

¼ tsp freshly ground black pepper

4 cups day-old, whole-grain bread cubes

½ cup fresh or canned pumpkin purée

1½ cups **From-Scratch Chicken Stock (see p100)** or low-sodium chicken stock

1. Select **Sauté**, and add the olive oil to the inner pot. Add the onion, sage, and thyme, kosher salt, and pepper. Sauté for 3 minutes, or until the onions are soft and translucent. Transfer to a large bowl and set aside.

2. Remove the inner pot from the base, wash in hot soapy water, and return to the base. Place the steam rack in the inner pot, and add 1 cup water.

3. Add the bread cubes and pumpkin to the onion mixture. Mix well. Add the chicken stock, ½ cup at a time, until the mixture is moist, but not saturated. (You may not need the full amount.)

4. Transfer the mixture to a 1-quart soufflé dish and loosely cover with aluminum foil. Carefully lower the dish into the inner pot. Preheat the oven to 400°F (204°C).

5. Cover, lock the lid, and flip the steam release handle to the sealing position. Select **Pressure Cook (High)**, and set the cook time for **10 minutes**. When the cook time is complete, quick release the pressure.

6. Remove the lid. Carefully remove the dish from the inner pot and transfer to the oven. Bake for 5–7 minutes, or until the top is golden brown. Serve warm.

Make this vegan by substituting vegetable broth for the chicken stock.

NUTRITION PER SERVING

Total fat **6g**	Cholesterol **0mg**	Carbohydrates **15g**	Sugars **3g**
Saturated fat **1g**	Sodium **293mg**	Dietary fiber **2g**	Protein **7g**

Honey-Glazed Carrots

Instead of being drenched in butter, these carrots are tossed in a lightly sweet honey sauce. Quick steaming the carrots helps preserve vitamins and antioxidants.

83 CALORIES PER SERVING

SERVES **4**
SERVING SIZE **1 cup**
PREP TIME **5 mins**
COOK TIME **10 mins**
TOTAL TIME **25 mins**

PROGRAM
Steam/Sauté

PRESSURE
High

RELEASE
Quick

1. Place the steam rack in the inner pot, and add the carrots and 1 cup water.

2. Cover, lock the lid, and flip the steam release handle to the sealing position. Select **Steam**, and set the cook time for **4 minutes**. When the cook time is complete, quick release the pressure.

3. Open the lid. Transfer the carrots to a medium bowl and set aside. Carefully remove the inner pot from the base, drain the water, and return the inner pot to the base.

4. Select **Sauté**, and add the coconut oil and honey to the inner pot. Heat until the glaze begins to sizzle.

5. Add the cooked carrots back to the pot, and season with a pinch of kosher salt. Toss gently to coat the carrots in the glaze.

6. Transfer to a serving bowl and allow to cool for 5 minutes before serving. Serve warm.

1lb (450g) carrots, peeled and chopped into bite-sized chunks
2 tsp coconut oil
1 tbsp honey
Kosher salt

To prevent overcooking, always quick release the pressure when cooking veggies.

NUTRITION PER SERVING

Total fat **3g**	Cholesterol **0mg**	Carbohydrates **15g**	Sugars **10g**
Saturated fat **2g**	Sodium **78mg**	Dietary fiber **3g**	Protein **1g**

Desserts

266 CALORIES PER SERVING

SERVES **4**
SERVING SIZE **1**
PREP TIME **10 mins**
COOK TIME **15 mins**
TOTAL TIME **45 mins**

Honey Cardamom Walnut Parfaits

These luscious parfaits taste amazing, and they're actually good for you! Spiced nuts, decadent white chocolate, and tangy kiwi will satisfy even the most powerful cravings.

 PROGRAM
Sauté/Pressure Cook

PRESSURE
High

RELEASE
Quick

¼ cup white chocolate chips

3 cups **Homemade Greek Yogurt (see p33)** or low-fat Greek yogurt

¾ cup walnuts

2 tbsp honey

½ tsp ground cardamom

Pinch kosher salt

½ cup water

3 kiwi, peeled and diced

1. Place the chocolate chips in a microwave-safe bowl. Microwave on high, in 30-second increments, until the chips are completely melted.

2. In a medium bowl, combine the Greek yogurt and melted chocolate. Gently fold the chocolate into the yogurt. Place in the refrigerator to chill for a minimum of 30 minutes, or up to overnight.

3. Select **Sauté**. Add the walnuts, honey, cardamom, and kosher salt to the inner pot, and toss gently to coat the nuts in the honey and spices. Press **Cancel** to turn off the heat, and then add the water.

4. Cover, lock the lid, and flip the steam release handle to the sealing position. Select **Pressure Cook (High)**, and set the cook time for **5 minutes**.

5. While the nuts are cooking, preheat the oven to 375°F (191°C), and line a large baking sheet with parchment paper.

6. When the cook time for the nuts is complete, quick release the pressure, remove the lid, and stir. Transfer the nuts to the prepared baking sheet and place in the oven to bake for 6–7 minutes. Once the baking time is complete, remove from the oven, and set aside to cool for about 10 minutes.

7. Assemble the parfaits by adding a layer of the chocolate and yogurt mixture in a small glass, followed by a layer of the nuts, and then a layer of the kiwi. Add a second layer of each ingredient to the glass. Repeat the process for the remaining servings. Serve immediately.

NUTRITION PER SERVING

Total fat **8g**	Cholesterol **0mg**	Carbohydrates **35g**	Sugars **30g**
Saturated fat **4g**	Sodium **116mg**	Dietary fiber **2g**	Protein **17g**

Cherries Jubilee

Cherries jubilee traditionally is served over ice cream, but this sweet and tangy sauce is served over fat-free vanilla frozen yogurt to create a light and delightful dessert.

219 CALORIES PER SERVING

SERVES **8**
SERVING SIZE **¼ cup**
PREP TIME **10 mins**
COOK TIME **10 mins**
TOTAL TIME **30 mins**

 PROGRAM
Pressure Cook

 PRESSURE
High

RELEASE
Quick

1. Combine the cherries, vegetable oil spread, brown sugar, kosher salt, and water in the inner pot. Stir gently.

2. Cover, lock the lid, and flip the steam release handle to the sealing position. Select **Pressure Cook (High)**, and set the cook time for **5 minutes**. When the cook time is complete, quick release the pressure.

3. Remove the lid. Select **Sauté**, and bring the ingredients to a simmer.

4. While the cherries are coming to a simmer, combine the cornstarch and brandy in a medium bowl. Mix well.

5. Add the cornstarch mixture to the pot and simmer for an additional 3–5 minutes, or until the mixture thickens. Once the mixture has thickened, press **Cancel** to turn off the heat, and add the lemon juice. Mix well, and allow to cool slightly.

6. Add ¾ cup of the frozen yogurt to a serving bowl, and top with ¼ cup of the cherries. Serve warm.

1lb (450g) frozen cherries
2 tsp vegetable oil spread
3 tbsp light brown sugar
Pinch kosher salt
¼ cup water
2 tsp cornstarch
2 tbsp brandy
2 tsp lemon juice
6 cups fat-free vanilla frozen yogurt

Cherries contain antioxidants, which can fight inflammation and also help lower blood pressure.

NUTRITION PER SERVING

| Total fat **1g** | Cholesterol **0mg** | Carbohydrates **44g** | Sugars **41g** |
| Saturated fat **0g** | Sodium **115mg** | Dietary fiber **1g** | Protein **5g** |

Rainbow Cheesecake

Reduced-fat cream cheese and Greek yogurt help lighten up this classic recipe, which was inspired by my mom (who makes the best darned cheesecake on the planet).

238 CALORIES PER SERVING

SERVES **10**
SERVING SIZE **1 slice**
PREP TIME **15 mins**
COOK TIME **1 hr 5 mins**
TOTAL TIME **7 hrs 30 mins**

 PROGRAM
Pressure Cook

 PRESSURE
Low

RELEASE
Natural

1. Preheat the oven to 350°F (177°C). In a medium bowl, combine the butter, graham cracker crumbs, and 1½ tsp of the sugar. Mix well.

2. Pour the mixture into a 7-inch (17.5cm) springform pan, and press the mixture down to form an even crust. Place in the oven to bake for 8 minutes, and then set aside to cool.

3. In a medium bowl, combine the cream cheese, reduced-fat cream cheese, and ⅔ cup of the sugar. Using a stand mixer with a paddle attachment or a hand mixer, mix on medium speed until the ingredients become light and fluffy, stopping periodically to scrape the sides of the bowl with a spatula.

4. Reduce the mixer speed to low, and begin adding the eggs, one at a time, followed by the Greek yogurt and vanilla. Mix well. Pour the mixture over the cooled crust, and cover loosely with aluminum foil.

5. Place the steam rack in the inner pot and add 1 cup water to the bottom of the pot. Carefully lower the pan onto the steam rack.

6. Cover, lock the lid, and flip the steam release handle to the sealing position. Select **Pressure Cook (Low)**, and set the cook time for **35 minutes**. When the cook time is complete, allow the pressure to release naturally (about 20 minutes).

7. Carefully remove the lid, lift the pan out of the pot, and set aside to cool. Once cooled, cover and place in the refrigerator to chill for a minimum of 6 hours.

8. Arrange fruit in a rainbow pattern on top before slicing. Serve chilled.

1 tbsp butter, melted

1 cup graham cracker crumbs

1½ tsp, plus ⅔ cup granulated sugar

8oz (225g) cream cheese, at room temperature

8oz (225g) ⅓-less-fat cream cheese, at room temperature

2 large eggs, at room temperature

⅓ cup **Homemade Greek Yogurt (see p33)** or low-fat Greek yogurt

2 tsp vanilla extract

Multi-colored fruit for topping (such as strawberries, clementines, banana, kiwi, blueberries, blackberries)

NUTRITION PER SERVING

Total fat **14g**	Cholesterol **73mg**	Carbohydrates **23g**	Sugars **17g**
Saturated fat **8g**	Sodium **256mg**	Dietary fiber **1g**	Protein **6g**

Peanut Butter Cheesecake Cups

199 CALORIES PER SERVING

MAKES **6**
SERVING SIZE **1**
PREP TIME **15 mins**
COOK TIME **35 mins**
TOTAL TIME **7 hrs**

This lighter, sweet-tooth-satisying treat uses perfect portions of lighter ingredients to create a creamy, decadent dessert that is guilt-free!

PROGRAM
Pressure Cook

 PRESSURE
Low

 RELEASE
Natural

⅓ cup sugar

4oz (110g) ⅓-less-fat cream cheese, at room temperature

4oz (110g) cream cheese, at room temperature

1 large egg, at room temperature

2 tbsp creamy peanut butter

½ tsp vanilla extract

6 tbsp whipped cream

1. Combine the sugar, reduced-fat cream cheese, and cream cheese in a large mixing bowl. Using a stand mixer with a paddle attachment or a hand mixer, mix on medium speed until the ingredients are light and fluffy, stopping the periodically to scrape the sides of the bowl with a spatula.

2. Adjust the mixer speed to low. Add the egg, followed by the peanut butter and vanilla. Mix until the ingredients are well combined.

3. Add equal amounts of the mixture to 6 ramekins, and cover each with aluminum foil.

4. Add 1 inch (2.5cm) of water to the inner pot, and then place 3 ramekins in the bottom of the pot. Place the steam rack over top of the ramekins, and place the remaining ramekins on the rack.

5. Cover, lock the lid, and flip the steam release handle to the sealing position. Select **Pressure Cook (Low)**, and set the cook time for **15 minutes**. When the cook time is complete, allow the pressure to release naturally (about 20 minutes).

6. Remove the lid. Using tongs, remove the ramekins from the pot, remove the foil, and set aside to cool to room temperature. Once cooled, cover the ramekins with plastic wrap and place in the refrigerator to chill for a minimum of 6 hours.

7. Once the cups are chilled, top each with 1 tablespoon whipped cream. Serve chilled.

NUTRITION PER SERVING

Total fat **14g**	Cholesterol **65mg**	Carbohydrates **14g**	Sugars **13g**
Saturated fat **6g**	Sodium **186mg**	Dietary fiber **0g**	Protein **5g**

Cinnamon-Spiked Rice Pudding

This rice pudding contains 200 fewer calories per serving than traditional rice pudding, and it's also higher in protein and fiber thanks to whole grain brown rice.

228 CALORIES PER SERVING

SERVES **6**
SERVING SIZE **¾ cup**
PREP TIME **10 mins**
COOK TIME **30 mins**
TOTAL TIME **50 mins**

PROGRAM
Pressure Cook

PRESSURE
High

RELEASE
Natural/Quick

1. Combine the rice, milk, kosher salt, and cinnamon stick in the inner pot.

2. Cover, lock the lid, and flip the steam release handle to the sealing position. Select **Pressure Cook (High)**, and set the cook time for **20 minutes**. Once the cook time is complete, allow the pressure to release naturally for 10 minutes, and then quick release the remaining pressure.

3. Remove the lid. Remove and discard the cinnamon stick, and then add the vanilla, ground cinnamon, condensed milk, and raisins. Stir well.

4. Transfer to serving bowls. Serve warm, or transfer to a sealable container, refrigerate, and serve chilled.

1 cup whole-grain brown rice
2 cups whole milk
Pinch kosher salt
1 cinnamon stick
1 tsp vanilla extract
½ tsp ground cinnamon
¼ cup sweetened condensed milk
¼ cup raisins

NUTRITION PER SERVING

Total fat **4g**	Cholesterol **15mg**	Carbohydrates **39g**	Sugars **16g**
Saturated fat **2g**	Sodium **81mg**	Dietary fiber **1g**	Protein **7g**

219 CALORIES
PER SERVING

SERVES **6**
SERVING SIZE **about ½ cup**
PREP TIME **20 mins**
COOK TIME **30 mins**
TOTAL TIME **1 hr 15 mins**

Coconut Crème Brulee

Instead of heavy cream, this crème brulee features whole milk and coconut milk to create a lighter, velvety-sweet version of one of my all-time favorite obsessions.

 PROGRAM
Pressure Cook

 PRESSURE
High

RELEASE
Natural/Quick

1 cup whole milk
1 tsp cornstarch
6 egg yolks
⅓ cup, plus 6 tsp granulated sugar
1 cup canned coconut milk
2 tsp vanilla extract
Fresh berries for serving

1. Place the steam rack in the inner pot, and add 1½ cups water. In a small bowl, combine the milk and cornstarch, and stir until the cornstarch is completely dissolved.

2. In a medium bowl, combine the egg yolks and ⅓ cup of the sugar. Whisk until well combined, and then whisk in the cornstarch mixture, followed by the coconut milk and vanilla.

3. Strain the mixture through a fine mesh sieve and into a large, 4-cup measuring cup. Pour equal amounts of the mixture into 6 medium ramekins and cover each with a small piece of aluminum foil. Place 3 ramekins on the steam rack.

4. Cover, lock the lid, and flip the steam release handle to the sealing position. Select **Pressure Cook (High)**, and set the cook time for **8 minutes**. Once the cook time is complete, allow the pressure to release naturally for 5 minutes, and then quick release the remaining pressure.

5. Remove the lid. Using tongs, remove the ramekins from pot, remove the foil, and set aside to cool. Repeat with the remaining ramekins. Once the ramekins have cooled, individually cover with plastic wrap and transfer to the refrigerator to chill for a minimum of 4 hours.

6. Preheat the broiler to high. Sprinkle 1 teaspoon sugar over top of each ramekin. Place the ramekins on a large sheet pan and broil for 1–2 minutes, or until the sugar melts and becomes slightly caramelized.

7. Remove from the oven and allow to cool slightly. Top each serving with fresh berries. Serve warm.

For richer coconut flavor, substitute coconut extract for the vanilla extract.

NUTRITION PER SERVING

Total fat **14g**	Cholesterol **189mg**	Carbohydrates **19g**	Sugars **18g**
Saturated fat **10g**	Sodium **31mg**	Dietary fiber **0g**	Protein **5g**

Nutella Pudding Cake

You'll absolutely swoon for this rich, decadent dessert that's made with only three simple ingredients and contains 6 grams of protein per serving.

 PROGRAM
Pressure Cook

 PRESSURE
High

RELEASE
Quick

½ cup Nutella hazelnut spread
1 egg, beaten
⅓ cup all-purpose flour
½ tsp confectioners' sugar
1 cup sliced strawberries

1. Spray a 6-inch (15.25cm) round baking dish with nonstick cooking spray. Place the steam rack in the inner pot, and add 1 cup water.

2. In a medium bowl, make the batter by combining the Nutella, egg, and flour. Mix well.

3. Pour the batter into the prepared baking dish. Loosely cover the dish with aluminum foil, and carefully lower into the pot.

4. Cover, lock the lid, and flip the steam release handle to the sealing position. Select **Pressure Cook (High)**, and set the cook time for **10 minutes**. When the cook time is complete, quick release the pressure.

5. Carefully remove the baking dish from the pot. Allow to cool for 5 minutes, and then dust with confectioners' sugar and top with strawberries. Slice into four equal-sized portions. Serve warm.

NUTRITION PER SERVING

Total fat **12g**	Cholesterol **47mg**	Carbohydrates **32g**	Sugars **23g**
Saturated fat **4g**	Sodium **33mg**	Dietary fiber **2g**	Protein **6g**

Warm Spiced Cider

Sweetened only with fruit, this warm and cozy beverage is a healthy and hydrating treat, and the perfect substitute for a sugary, high-calorie dessert on a chilly evening.

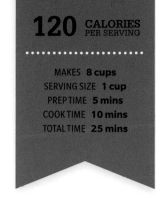

120 **CALORIES** PER SERVING

MAKES **8 cups**
SERVING SIZE **1 cup**
PREP TIME **5 mins**
COOK TIME **10 mins**
TOTAL TIME **25 mins**

 PROGRAM **Pressure Cook**

 PRESSURE **High**

 RELEASE **Quick**

1. Combine the cider, cinnamon sticks, cloves, cardamom pods, and lemon slices in the inner pot.

2. Cover, lock the lid, and flip the steam release handle to the sealing position. Select **Pressure Cook (High)**, and set the cook time for **10 minutes**. When the cook time is complete, quick release the pressure.

3. Select **Keep Warm**, and ladle the cider into mugs for serving. Serve warm.

8 cups apple cider
2 cinnamon sticks
1 tsp whole cloves
1 tbsp cardamom pods
1 lemon, sliced

NUTRITION PER SERVING

| Total fat **120g** | Cholesterol **0mg** | Carbohydrates **28g** | Sugars **26g** |
| Saturated fat **0g** | Sodium **0mg** | Dietary fiber **0g** | Protein **0g** |

Poached Cinnamon Pears

This elegant, delicate treat is high in fiber, low in sugar, and ready in about 30 minutes. Substituting fruit juice for sugar helps keep the sugar content low.

150 CALORIES PER SERVING

SERVES **4**
SERVING SIZE **1**
PREP TIME **10 mins**
COOK TIME **16 mins**
TOTAL TIME **35 mins**

PROGRAM
Pressure Cook

PRESSURE
High

RELEASE
Natural

1. Combine the fruit juice, lemon juice, cinnamon stick, star anise, and water in the inner pot.

2. Peel the pears, but leave the stems on. Immediately place the pears in the liquid. (If there's not enough liquid to cover the pears, add more water, one tablespoon at a time, until the liquid completely covers the pears.)

3. Cover, lock the lid, and flip the steam release handle to the sealing position. Select **Pressure Cook (High)**, and set the cook time for **6 minutes**. When the cook time is complete, allow the pressure to release naturally (about 10 minutes).

4. Using a slotted spoon, carefully transfer the pears to a serving platter. Serve warm, or transfer the cooled pears to a sealable container and chill in the refrigerator for a minimum of 3 hours before serving.

3 cups 100% apple or white grape juice
Juice of 1 lemon
1 cinnamon stick
1 whole star anise
3½ cups water
4 pears (Anjou or Bartlett varieties)

NUTRITION PER SERVING

Total fat **0g**	Cholesterol **0mg**	Carbohydrates **36g**	Sugars **25g**
Saturated fat **0g**	Sodium **2mg**	Dietary fiber **6g**	Protein **1g**

Bananas Foster

This healthier take on the famous New Orleans dessert highlights the natural sweetness of banana, and is served with frozen yogurt in place of ice cream.

· ·

 PROGRAM
Pressure Cook

 PRESSURE
High

RELEASE
Quick

3 ripe bananas, cut into
 1-inch-thick (2.5cm) slices

2 tsp vegetable oil spread

2 tbsp lightly packed
 light brown sugar

Pinch kosher salt

⅓ cup water

2 cups frozen vanilla yogurt

¼ cup chopped walnuts

1. Combine the banana slices, vegetable oil spread, brown sugar, kosher salt, and water in the inner pot. Stir gently.

2. Cover, lock the lid, and flip the steam release handle to the sealing position. Select **Pressure Cook (High)**, and set the cook time for **1 minute**. When the cook time is complete, quick release the pressure.

3. Remove the lid. Transfer the bananas and sauce to a medium bowl, and let cool slightly.

4. Add ½ cup frozen yogurt to a serving bowl. Top with ¼ cup of the bananas and sauce, and 1 tablespoon of the walnuts. Repeat with the remaining servings. Serve warm.

NUTRITION PER SERVING

Total fat **7g**	Cholesterol **4mg**	Carbohydrates **34g**	Sugars **28g**
Saturated fat **1g**	Sodium **120mg**	Dietary fiber **1g**	Protein **5g**

White Hot Chocolate

This rich, comforting treat includes a dose of bone-building calicum, and is lighter than similar drinks that can tip the scales at nearly 350 calories per serving.

180 CALORIES PER SERVING

SERVES **3**
SERVING SIZE **6 fl oz (175ml)**
PREP TIME **2 mins**
COOK TIME **5 mins**
TOTAL TIME **15 mins**

 PROGRAM **Yogurt**

 PRESSURE **none**

 RELEASE **none**

1. Add the milk to the inner pot.

2. Cover and lock the lid, but leave the steam release handle in the venting position. Select **Yogurt (Boil)**.

3. When the boil cycle is complete, remove the lid, carefully remove the inner pot from the base, and transfer to a heat-resistant surface.

4. Add the vanilla and chocolate chips. Whisk the ingredients vigorously until the chocolate is melted, and the milk is frothy.

5. Ladle into mugs. Serve hot.

2 cups whole milk
1 tsp vanilla extract
¼ cup white chocolate chips

For a special holiday flavor treat, add a small splash of peppermint extract.

NUTRITION PER SERVING

Total fat **9g**	Cholesterol **13mg**	Carbohydrates **21g**	Sugars **17g**
Saturated fat **7g**	Sodium **103mg**	Dietary fiber **0g**	Protein **5g**

Pumpkin Chip Tea Cake

Pumpkin and chocolate is one of my favorite flavor combinations! The applesauce and pumpkin in this deliciously moist cake help cut back the fat.

 PROGRAM
Pressure Cook

 PRESSURE
High

RELEASE
Natural/Quick

1 cup all-purpose flour
1 cup wheat flour
1½ tsp baking powder
½ tsp baking soda
½ tsp ground cinnamon
½ tsp kosher salt
1 cup granulated sugar
1 large egg, beaten
¼ cup canola oil
½ cup applesauce
1 cup low-fat milk
1 tsp vanilla extract
1 cup canned pumpkin purée
½ cup semi-sweet
  chocolate chips, divided

1. In a large bowl, combine the all-purpose flour, wheat flour, baking powder, baking soda, cinnamon, kosher salt, and sugar. Whisk well to combine.

2. Add the egg, canola oil, applesauce, milk, vanilla, and pumpkin purée to the bowl. Mix until well combined, and then fold in the chocolate chips.

3. Spray a 4-cup mini bundt pan with nonstick cooking spray. Add the batter to the pan.

4. Place the steam rack in the inner pot, and add 1 cup water to the bottom of the pot. Place the bundt pan on the steam rack, and loosely cover with aluminum foil.

5. Cover, lock the lid, and flip the steam release handle to the sealing position. Select **Pressure Cook (High)**, and set the cook time for **30 minutes**. When the cook time is complete, allow the pressure to release naturally for 10 minutes, and then quick release the remaining pressure.

6. Remove the lid, and carefully transfer the pan to a wire rack to cool.

7. Once the cake has cooled, cut it into 4 equal-sized slices. Serve warm.

For a different flavor, substitute ½ cup fresh cranberries for the chocolate chips.

NUTRITION PER SERVING

Total fat **8g**	Cholesterol **16mg**	Carbohydrates **42g**	Sugars **25g**
Saturated fat **2g**	Sodium **178mg**	Dietary fiber **3g**	Protein **4g**

Dark Chocolate Fondue

The gentle heat of the Instant Pot is perfect for tempering chocolate! Using a high-quality, antioxidant-rich dark chocolate helps make this decadent treat healthier.

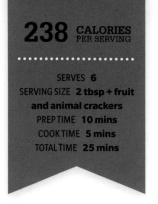 PROGRAM
Pressure Cook

 PRESSURE
High

 RELEASE
Quick

6oz (170g) 70% cacao dark chocolate, chopped
¼ cup heavy cream

For serving:
12 medium strawberries
2 bananas, thickly sliced
1 cup animal crackers
2 clementine oranges, segmented

1. Place the steam rack in the inner pot, and add 1 cup water to the bottom of the pot.

2. Fill two medium ramekins each with 3 ounces (85g) of the chocolate, and 2 tablespoons of the heavy cream. Loosely cover each ramekin with aluminum foil, and place on the steam rack.

3. Cover, lock the lid, and flip the steam release handle to the sealing position. Select **Pressure Cook (High)**, and set the cook time for **5 minutes**. When the cook time is complete, quick release the pressure.

4. Remove the lid. Using tongs, carefully transfer the ramekins to a serving platter, remove and discard the foil, and gently stir until the ingredients are well blended.

5. Serve warm, with fresh fruit and animal crackers served on the side, and bamboo skewers for dipping.

NUTRITION PER SERVING

Total fat **11g**	Cholesterol **13mg**	Carbohydrates **35g**	Sugars **23g**
Saturated fat **7g**	Sodium **54mg**	Dietary fiber **3g**	Protein **2g**

Peach Cherry Cobbler

This lightly sweet cobbler contains no added sugar and is sweetened only with fruit and fruit juice. The crust compliments the juicy peaches and cherries.

224 CALORIES PER SERVING

SERVES **4**
SERVING SIZE **1 cup**
PREP TIME **10 mins**
COOK TIME **18 mins**
TOTAL TIME **45 mins**

PROGRAM
Pressure Cook

PRESSURE
High

RELEASE
Natural

1. Reserve ¼ cup of the peach canning liquid in a small bowl. Add the cherries, peaches, and remaining canning liquid to the inner pot.

2. In a small bowl, combine the lemon juice, cornstarch, and reserved canning liquid. Stir well, and then add to the pot.

3. In a medium bowl, combine the flour, baking powder, baking soda, kosher salt, and butter. Using a fork or pastry cutter, mash the ingredients until the butter is fully incorporated into the dry ingredients.

4. Add the buttermilk to the bowl, and mix until a loose, sticky dough is formed. (If the mixture is too dry, add more buttermilk, 1 tbsp at a time, until the desired consistency is reached.)

5. Using a spoon, place large dollops of the biscuit dough on top of the fruit. Loosely cover the inner pot with a piece of aluminum foil.

6. Cover, lock the lid, and flip the steam release handle to the sealing position. Select **Pressure Cook (High)**, and set the cook time for **8 minutes**. When the cook time is complete, allow the pressure to release naturally (about 10 minutes).

7. Remove the lid, discard the foil, and carefully remove the inner pot from the base and transfer to a heat-safe surface. Allow the cobbler to cool and thicken for 10 minutes before spooning into serving bowls. Serve warm.

15 oz (420g) can sliced peaches, packed in 100% fruit juice
2 cups frozen cherries
2 tbsp freshly squeezed lemon juice
1 tsp cornstarch
½ cup all-purpose flour
½ tsp baking powder
⅛ tsp baking soda
¼ tsp kosher salt
1½ tbsp cold unsalted butter, diced
¼ cup low-fat buttermilk

This is delicious served with a small scoop of vanilla frozen yogurt!

NUTRITION PER SERVING

Total fat **4g**	Cholesterol **12mg**	Carbohydrates **43g**	Sugars **28g**
Saturated fat **3g**	Sodium **184mg**	Dietary fiber **3g**	Protein **4g**

Caramel Popcorn Crunch

This is my go-to snack for a crowd of hungry kids; it's sweet and salty, and provides some healthy fats as well as whole grains. (Yes, popcorn is a whole grain!)

200 **CALORIES** PER SERVING

MAKES **8 cups**
SERVING SIZE **1 cup**
PREP TIME **15 mins**
COOK TIME **45 mins**
TOTAL TIME **1 hr 30 mins**

PROGRAM
Pressure Cook

PRESSURE
High

RELEASE
Quick

1. Place the steam rack in the inner pot. Place the popcorn kernels in a medium brown paper lunch bag, fold the top closed, and microwave on high for 2 minutes and 15 seconds, or until the popping begins to slow. Set aside.

2. Pour the condensed milk into a sealable glass canning jar, seal tightly, and place the jar on the steam rack. Add enough warm tap water to the inner pot to reach the same level as the condensed milk in the jar.

3. Cover, lock the lid, and flip the steam release handle to the sealing position. Select **Pressure Cook (High)**, and set the cook time for **35 minutes**. When the cook time is complete, quick release the pressure.

4. Remove the lid. Wait 10 minutes before carefully transferring the jar from the inner pot to a heat-resistant surface. When the jar is cool enough to handle, remove the lid, and stir the sauce.

5. Preheat the oven to 325°F (163°C) and line a large baking sheet with parchment paper. Spread the popcorn, cereal, and peanuts across the baking sheet. Evenly drizzle the caramel sauce across the corn, and then season with the sea salt.

6. Bake for 8 minutes, and then remove from the oven and allow to cool. Once cool, sprinkle the confectioners' sugar over top of the popcorn. Toss gently to evenly coat the popcorn in the sugar.

7. Serve immediately, or transfer to an airtight container and store at room temperature for up to 2 days.

¼ cup unpopped popcorn kernels

¾ cup sweetened condensed milk

1 cup Honey Nut Chex cereal (or other gluten-free honey nut cereal)

¾ cup honey-roasted peanuts

1 tsp sea salt

2 tsp confectioners' sugar

NUTRITION PER SERVING

Total fat **8g**	Cholesterol **8mg**	Carbohydrates **28g**	Sugars **19g**
Saturated fat **2g**	Sodium **358mg**	Dietary fiber **2g**	Protein **6g**

Index

SYMBOLS

Penguin Random House

Publisher Mike Sanders
Senior Editor Brook Farling
Book Designer Lindsay Dobbs
Art Director William Thomas
Photographer Kelley Jordan Schuyler
Food Stylist Savannah Norris
Proofreader Lisa Starnes
Indexer Brad Herriman

First American Edition, 2018
Published in the United States by DK Publishing
6081 E. 82nd Street, Indianapolis, Indiana 46250

Copyright © 2018 Dorling Kindersley Limited
DK, a Division of Penguin Random House LLC
18 19 20 21 22   10 9 8 7 6 5 4 3 2 1
001–309808–October/2018

A catalog record for this book
is available from the Library of Congress.
ISBN 978-1-4654-7663-0
Library of Congress Catalog Number: 2018933876

DK books are available at special discounts when purchased
in bulk for sales promotions, premiums, fund-raising, or educational
use. For details, contact: DK Publishing Special Markets, 345 Hudson
Street, New York, New York 10014
SpecialSales@dk.com

Printed and bound in China

All images © Dorling Kindersley Limited
For further information see: www.dkimages.com

A WORLD OF IDEAS:
SEE ALL THERE IS TO KNOW

www.dk.com